HOW TO MARKET YOURSELF

In this Series

Other titles in preparation

MARKET YOURSELF

A practical guide to winning at work

Ian Phillipson

How To Books

By the same author

How to Do Your Own PR
How to Start Word Processing
How to Work from Home

Cartoons by Mike Flanagan

British Library Cataloguing-in-Publication data
A catalogue record for this book is available from the British Library.

© Copyright 1995 by Ian Phillipson.

First published in 1995 by How To Books Ltd, Plymbridge House, Estover Road, Plymouth PL6 7PZ, United Kingdom.
Tel: (01752) 735251/695745. Fax: (01752) 695699.
Telex: 45635.

Note: The material contained in this book is set out in good faith for general guidance and no liability can be accepted for loss or expense incurred as a result of relying in particular circumstances on statements made in the book. The laws and regulations are complex and liable to change, and readers should check the current position with the relevant authorities before making personal arrangements.

Typeset by Kestrel Data, Exeter.
Printed and bound in Great Britain by The Cromwell Press, Broughton Gifford, Melksham, Wiltshire.

Contents

List of Illustrations

9

Preface

In our less than perfect world sometimes being the best person for the job or for a promotion simply isn't good enough. Others have to know that too. However, some people just don't know how to show themselves off in the best light and because of that they frequently lose out to those who do, despite being less well qualified or experienced.

For the 'losers', working life can be tremendously frustrating as they become locked into a job or a career path for years on end, watching others pass them by and climbing ladders ahead of them.

But while some people are naturally good at marketing themselves to others, there are techniques and methods that you can use even if you aren't a 'natural'. However, to become better at marketing yourself you will have to put in time and effort—few things in this life come easy. But it will be worth it not only to improve your career prospects, but to make your work more rewarding and fun.

Of course, you can benefit from acquiring self-marketing skills even if you don't have any particular job or career ambitions at the moment. In fact, there is a lot to be said for making changes before you need to, then you won't feel so under time pressure when an opportunity arises. And once you have the skills you can use them in your everyday life to create a better self-image.

So the best of luck in creating a 'new you' that will be better equipped to succeed.

Ian Phillipson

IS THIS YOU?

Woman returner	First time jobseeker	Secretary
Ambitious executive	Unemployed	A partner
Part-time employee	Office junior	Manager
Full-time employee	Self-employed	Retiree
Middle manager	Volunteer staff	Telephonist
Part-time helper	Community worker	Typist
Personnel assistant	School leaver	Receptionist
Personal assistant	College leaver	Redundant
Holiday employee	Admin assistant	Clerk
Business person	Wages clerk	Estate agent
Computer operator	Trainee manager	Freelance
Public speaker	Press spokesperson	Organiser
Support staff	Financial consultant	Teacher
Data inputter	Local councillor	Fundraiser
Retail staff	Travel agent	Publican
Charity organiser	Event organiser	Hotelier
	Shop assistant	Homeworker

1
Do You Need To Market Yourself?

WHAT'S MARKETING?

Self-marketing is a systematic approach to the promotion of a very important product, you. It is something that you can use to help find your first job, to obtain promotion with your existing company, to move into a new job or to increase business if you have your own company. It is **personal public relations**, creating an image for yourself that presents you in the most positive light.

However, marketing anything, whether it is you or a washing machine, *isn't* the same as selling.

At one time businesses weren't really that interested in their customers and what they wanted. They simply made a product or offered a service and then tried to sell it even if it wasn't what customers wanted. Prospective customers and clients either bought because there was nothing more suitable available, or were forced into buying through high pressure tactics, deceitful advertising claims and other desperate measures.

Though all of these things still go on today and some companies still live in the past, most have learned the value of marketing.

Marketing makes life much easier for everyone because it involves finding out what people want and then offering it to them and this can be done either for products and services or for a person.

Consequently marketing yourself is a two-part process. The first part concentrates not on you, but on the people you want to reach, **your market**, because only when you've found out what your market wants can you create the product (you) that they want to buy.

Seeing yourself as a product
In self-marketing, you are the product on offer to the market and

you have to see yourself as that. If this sounds rather 'inhuman' and clinical, it isn't meant to be. Everyone markets themselves to a greater or lesser extent every day. Whenever you comb your hair, put on perfume or aftershave, or are polite to others, you are in the business of self-marketing, trying to produce an image you want others to see. All this book suggests is that you do this on a more formal and organised level.

It makes sense to package yourself in the best light as generally everyone is 'drawn' to attractive products. But that doesn't mean you have to be physically attractive to be effective in your self-marketing as largely you will be appealing to the many different aspects of human nature.

Self-marketing doesn't require you to change your personality or to become another person. Many of the changes that you can make to increase your marketability are simple and easy to put into effect, though having examined yourself you may find that a more radical overhaul is required. That is up to you. And successful self-marketing involves paying not only attention to detail but also more major and basic aspects. Remember, you are your most important asset.

One advantage of learning to market yourself is that you will begin to look at other people with a keener eye, and notice how they see themselves and how they are trying to influence you. That can be valuable information to have.

WHY MARKET YOURSELF?

What is the point of marketing yourself? After all you've got by so far without bothering. However, from time to time everyone has to market themselves. If you are trying to attract a boyfriend or girlfriend you have to market yourself. If you are after a new job or a promotion you have to market yourself, and it's never too early or too late to learn how.

The modern world is becoming increasingly competitive with more and more people after the same job, more and more people not wanting to be left behind, more and more people wanting to have all the benefits of modern society. This means that we are all to an extent in competition with other people, for new jobs, promotion and business. Indeed, for the younger person knowing how to market yourself can be an absolutely crucial skill because, unlike someone older, they generally have fewer skills and less experience to offer.

What is more the world is changing faster and faster. Forty years ago there were no software programmers, computer operators, desktop publishers, mobile phone suppliers, or multimedia designers—these jobs just didn't exist. In 40 years' time which of today's jobs will have gone the way of lamplighters, makers of spats, ratcatchers and the like?

All this change means there are also a great number of opportunities opening up for those who are willing to go after them and grasp them. But while there are a lot of opportunities you still have to make them yours and the better able you are to market yourself the more opportunities you'll grasp.

It is also important to remember that very often it isn't the best person for a job who gets it, but the person who markets themselves sufficiently well that others *think* they are the best person for the job.

You don't need to be highly intelligent, have an outrageously outgoing personality or be stunningly attractive to market yourself well. Anyone can learn to do it if they are willing to make the effort, make the necessary changes, acquire new skills and are willing to see themselves as something of a product that can be modified and revised.

WHO NEEDS THIS BOOK?

How to Market Yourself is for anyone who wants to present themselves in a better light whether they are redundant, starting back to work after a long period off, self employed, first time job seekers, women returners, start up business people, already in a career, part-time workers, full-time workers, young, old, male and female, well educated and the less well qualified. *How to Market Yourself* is for all of these.

Ultimately no book can give a formula for self-marketing success, but it can point you in the right direction. Whether you succeed or not will depend on the work and thought that you are willing to put in.

Whatever stage of your career you are at you can always do with some self-marketing and this book will help show you how, especially if you don't have much work or business experience. But

How to Market Yourself is not a book on how to get a job. There are already many very good books on that subject which cover in detail how to answer interview questions and produce job winning CVs. While some parts of these topics are covered here, *How to Market Yourself* is more about making a more marketable commodity.

CHECKLIST—DO YOU NEED TO MARKET YOURSELF?

Do you work in a competitive environment where your performance is frequently compared with that of others?   Yes/No

Do you frequently just miss out to other people when going for promotion or a new job?   Yes/No

Even though you want another job have you been stuck in the same one for longer than you want?   Yes/No

Do you just let life happen to you rather than having a plan for what you want out of life?   Yes/No

Do you frequently compare yourself with other people and wish you were them?   Yes/No

Do you think that people should take you as they find you? If they don't like you then that's their hard luck?   Yes/No

Do you find that if you are in a crowd you tend to be pushed out to the edge and forgotten about?   Yes/No

If you answered yes to most of those questions then the chances are that you need to market yourself more. In highly competitive companies and organisations there is often very little to choose between two people when it comes to promotion so attention to detail becomes ever more important.

Do you market yourself already?

Can you think of five occasions when you have marketed yourself in the last year? Write them down here:

1 . . . .
2 . . . .
3 . . . .
4 . . . .
5 . . . .

Why did you have to market yourself on these occasions? Write down the reasons:

1 . . . .
2 . . . .
3 . . . .
4 . . . .
5 . . . .

How exactly did you market yourself?

1 . . . .
2 . . . .
3 . . . .
4 . . . .
5 . . . .

Think of five occasions when you lost out because you didn't present yourself in the best light through inadequate self-marketing:

1 . . . .
2 . . . .
3 . . . .
4 . . . .
5 . . . .

The downside of self-marketing

There is one potential problem with self-marketing and that is that you can be seen as pushy and out for everything you can get. That may not always be damaging, especially if you only intend to be with a company or involved in a situation temporarily, but it can be highly counter-productive if you are looking to make your way to the top of a large company, which could take years. Therefore you generally have to strike a balance between your own ambitions and the appearance you give to others.

WHEN TO MARKET YOURSELF

You can market yourself at virtually any time you want. How much self-marketing you do is down to personal preference and what you want to achieve. If you are in job search then you will probably end up marketing yourself quite intensively for two or three months and then taking a breather while you settle into your new position. If you are already in work and wanting to move up the corporate ladder then your self-marketing will probably be a slower, on-going process.

How quickly can you market yourself?

You can start marketing yourself immediately, though while some of your efforts will bear fruit almost instantaneously or within a few weeks, it may take years for you to reap the full benefits of other parts of your self-marketing strategy.

Really you should start thinking of self-marketing as a series of steps, each one a goal in itself, but leading on to bigger and better goals which may be some time down the road.

DEVELOPING THE RIGHT APPROACH

Marketing yourself is quite a hard thing to do as it is something that doesn't just happen, but requires effort on your part. In fact, you are rather like a film star with a posse of publicists and promotions people all pushing to get her name in front of the public, only you don't have all of those people to help you—you have to do everything yourself and as yet you are not a star. All this means that you are the one who has to make things happen for yourself.

If you just sit back there is no hope. Of course, you might get some lucky breaks, but for the most part you will just drift along taking what life and your career dish out. As you are reading this book presumably you aren't satisfied with that.

If you are to market yourself successfully then you should be positive about what life has to offer and about what you can achieve. If you think you will never amount to anything nor make a success of yourself then that is exactly what will happen. So **be positive**. Positive people are winners. Negative people are losers.

If you are still not sure that you can market yourself in such a way that makes a difference to your life, look at these examples from history of 'no-hopers' succeeding: playwright George Bernard Shaw was considered to be a bad speller; American scientist Benjamin Franklin was poor at maths; highly successful horror novelist Edgar Allan Poe was expelled from school; and Albert Einstein, whose Theory of Relativity elevated him to international fame, was considered slow at school! It just goes to show that ugly ducklings do turn into swans.

CASE HISTORIES

Lynda lets others get the credit

Lynda has been working in the administration department of a pump manufacturer for the last five years. She works hard, is efficient and has a very good in-depth knowledge of the company and its procedures. Now a possible chance of promotion has come which Lynda wants very much. But though she is very well qualified for the position, she is not very good at marketing herself. And though her colleagues know what she is capable of, Lynda is rather modest and often lets others take the credit for her efforts and work, even when they aren't actually trying to do this. What is more, she has a rather dowdy appearance and isn't as neat as she could be—which suggests that she may not be precise and careful in her work. Inevitably someone else, Karen, is also after the promotion but, unlike Lynda, she makes a special effort to market herself by employing many of the techniques found in this book. The result, after careful interviewing, is that Karen is given the job. Lynda takes the disappointment with good grace and smiles as best she can when workmates say 'never mind, you were the best person for that job'. Lynda knows it too, but as with many people, all other things being equal the person with poor self-marketing skills has lost out to someone who is better at it.

Thomas takes a grip on life

Thomas is a purchasing manager for a large multinational company in the south of England. He is bright, intelligent and good at his job. However, he also is not very good at self-marketing—in fact his problem is that he has really never even thought about it. The result is that he has no plan for improving his situation and circumstances, even though he is ambitious. He is rather like the old fashioned company that makes things nobody wants but insists potential customers need them nevertheless. If only Thomas thought about marketing himself he would soon notice a difference in his working and private life.

2
How Good a Product are You?

FINDING OUT ABOUT YOURSELF

This is going to be something of a hard work chapter, because you'll be expected to answer a lot of questions about yourself: the way you look, the way you behave, your personality and your character. You should try to answer the questions as truthfully as you can. Think of this as being a job interview you're conducting on yourself. Of course, you can deceive yourself if you want. No one else will be hurt by that but you.

The purpose of this chapter is to help you build up a picture about yourself, rather like doing market research about yourself. It isn't an in-depth psychological test, but by the end of the chapter you should have a better idea of what you are good at and what you are not. Even if the question seems simple, still try and work out why it is being asked and what your answer says about you.

This may be the very first time that you have thought about exactly who you are, so spend an hour or so working through this assessment. It will be worth it in the end.

The questions are divided into groups to give you a better idea of what they are trying to find out about you.

How organised are you?

Are you able to get done the things you have to do?　　Yes/No

Do you do jobs when they have to be done rather than putting them off?　　Yes/No

Are you punctual and well able to keep appointments?　　Yes/No

Do you complete homework, college or work projects on time?　　Yes/No

Do you finish these in plenty of time without rushing
to do it at the last minute?   Yes/No

Do you plan the things that you have to do?   Yes/No

Do you organize systems for doing things, either for
yourself or others?   Yes/No

Do you plan what you are going to do in the day?   Yes/No

Do you make a list of the things you want or have
to do?   Yes/No

Do you write shopping lists?   Yes/No

When you are going on holiday do you make a list
of the things that you have to take with you?   Yes/No

Do you buy others birthday presents well ahead
of time?   Yes/No

Do you do your Christmas shopping early enough so
as to avoid the rush?   Yes/No

Are you the one that organises parties and events in
the family or at work?   Yes/No

How motivated are you?

If you need a new skill, perhaps for a job or hobby,
do you do something about it, have you gone out and
acquired the new skill?   Yes/No

Do you normally find you have enough energy to do
what you want to do?   Yes/No

Do you spend a lot of your spare time slumped in front
of the television?   Yes/No

Do you have a lot of stamina?   Yes/No

Do you make the time to play sports?   Yes/No

Do you train for any sports regularly? Yes/No

Do you find it fairly easy to do things on your own? Yes/No

Do you work on your own? Yes/No

Do you like always to have others around you? Yes/No

When you sit down to do something can you keep on doing it no matter what the distractions? Yes/No

You are in the middle of an urgent job and a friend drops by. Can you tell them to come back later when you have finished? Yes/No

Do you watch favourite television programmes rather than finish off jobs that need to be done, but which you don't like? Yes/No

Have you ever worked for longer than you needed to help someone out? Yes/No

Do you think that you are lazy? Yes/No

Do you think that you are hardworking? Yes/No

When you start something do you always finish it whenever humanly possible? Yes/No

Do you do any endurance sports like cross country, marathon running or the triathlon? Yes/No

Are you a risk taker?
Are you able to take risks? Yes/No

Are you someone who likes to try out new sports, activities, foods and restaurants? Yes/No

How well do you communicate?
Do people say that you talk well? Yes/No

If someone asked you to explain the plot of a television programme that you saw last night, could you do it quickly and easily?   Yes/No

Can you persuade others to do things that you want to do?   Yes/No

Are you able to give others good reasons why they should do what you want them to do?   Yes/No

You understand something, but someone else doesn't. Could you explain it to them in an interesting way that would help them understand?   Yes/No

How well do you get on with others?
Do you think that you get on well with other people?   Yes/No

Can you organise and supervise others so that they do a good job?   Yes/No

Have you ever sold anything to anyone?   Yes/No

Do you always want to be going out?   Yes/No

How decisive are you?
Are you good at making decisions?   Yes/No

Would you say that you are decisive?   Yes/No

Do you make decisions very often?   Yes/No

Do you put off making big decisions?   Yes/No

When you make a decision is it generally right?   Yes/No

Are you willing to learn?
Can you make the effort to learn new things?   Yes/No

Can you find out information when you need it?   Yes/No

Have you used a library recently?   Yes/No

Are you a planner?

Do you plan ahead?   Yes/No

Are you good at spotting potential problems?   Yes/No

How adaptable are you?

Can you do more than one thing at once?   Yes/No

Do you consider yourself flexible and adaptable?   Yes/No

How creative are you?

Do you think of yourself as being creative?   Yes/No

Do others say you've got a good imagination?   Yes/No

Do you do crosswords and puzzles?   Yes/No

Do you watch quiz programmes on TV?   Yes/No

Do you come up with new ideas frequently?   Yes/No

Do you do anything creative such as write, paint,
or play music?   Yes/No

How do you handle pressure?

Do you think you can cope with pressure?   Yes/No

If you have a problem is your first instinct to run
away from it?   Yes/No

Are you able to fight this and face the problem?   Yes/No

When others are under pressure do you take some of
it on yourself to try and help them out?   Yes/No

Having worked through the questionnaire, try and find someone
else to answer the same questions about you.

WHO ARE YOU?

Like most people you will have your own particular thoughts on the kind of person you are, but have you ever made those thoughts concrete, by sitting down and writing them out? No? Well, now is the time to do just that. Take the next ten to 20 minutes to put all these thoughts about yourself on paper. What do you think your strengths and weaknesses are? What type of personality do you have? Are you able to get on with people? Let such questions roll through your mind. The more you can think of the better because it will give you a fuller idea of your character. You don't need to spend a great deal of time trying to get the words, spelling or grammar right.

If you have the courage it's worth showing your self-description to your family and friends. Do they think you have got it right? If not then why not? Getting their input is valuable for two reasons. First, knowing that your assessment is going to come under the scrutiny of others means that you are less likely to indulge in wishful thinking about the way you would like to be rather than the way you are. And second, it also demonstrates that the way you see yourself is not always the way that others see you. That is a very important lesson when you are marketing yourself.

If you don't actually want others to see what you have written then ask them to write down their thoughts about you and then compare the two—your description and theirs. Where are the points of difference? If you violently disagree with something the other person has written, don't immediately fly off the handle. Rather ask why they think that about you and then consider whether they are right or not. This is truth time.

If you have answered yes to most of the questions asked above (and the input from another person will help prove that you haven't been deceiving yourself) then you are probably already quite well equipped to market yourself very effectively. Indeed, you probably do quite a lot of self-marketing already.

However, if you have answered no to a lot of the questions, then you will be highlighting potential areas of weakness. If you seem to have quite a few of these, don't worry. You can change matters. The important thing at this stage is not to be overwhelmed by the amount of work you might have to do on yourself. Making personal changes can be difficult for many people, but you will only start making a change if you do something. Just waiting for change won't make it happen.

Action point

Think about the people you mix with. Since we generally like and feel comfortable with people like ourselves, what are they like? How do they dress, behave and act? This will often say something about ourselves, or at least about part of the image that we are portraying to the rest of the world. Write down in 100 words what your friends are generally like, then ask yourself whether you are like them. Don't think too deeply about this, but put down your initial reactions:

WHAT WORDS BEST DESCRIBE YOU?

Below is a list of descriptive words. Choose the five that most closely describe you and rank them in order. Then choose the five that describe you least and rank them in order.

Energetic	Youthful	Old-fashioned	Creative
Capable	Efficient	Powerful	Disciplined
Reliable	Hardworking	Clever	Attractive
Professional	Ambitious	Mature	Co-operative
Assertive	Intelligent	Thoughtful	Intuitive
Friendly	Communicative	Cynical	Adaptable
Understanding	Forthright	Wishy-washy	Principled

Again get your friends and family to do the same about you. Compare their list with yours.

If someone were to ask you how you would describe yourself in one sentence what would you say?

. . . .
. . . .

If someone asked you how you would *like* to describe yourself in one sentence, what would you say?

. . . .
. . . .

You die at the ripe old age of 102, knocked down by a bus as you jog across the road. You have had a long, successful and productive life. In not more than 100 words, how would you like your obituary to read?

. . . .
. . . .

WHO DO YOU GET ON WITH?

It would be miraculous if we got on equally well with everyone, and of course we don't. There are some people with whom we seem to strike up a natural rapport. And when you have a rapport with people you are likely to have more influence over them and they are likely to treat you more favourably. Therefore it makes sense to strike up good relations with those people who can help you most. Write down the names of four people that you get on best with?

1 . . . .
2 . . . .
3 . . . .
4 . . . .

What about these people enables you to get on well with them?

1 . . . .
2 . . . .
3 . . . .
4 . . . .

Write down the names of four people that you get on least well with:

1 . . . .
2 . . . .
3 . . . .
4 . . . .

What about these people causes you to get on poorly with them?

1 . . . .
2 . . . .
3 . . . .
4 . . . .

If you know the type of people you get on well with you will be able to identify them in any company you work for and then easily build a rapport with them. On the other hand, if you know the type of people who rub you up the wrong way, you will be able to take this into consideration when dealing with them, and hopefully more easily control your temper and irritation.

SUMMARY

This may have been the very first time that you have had to look at yourself in such great detail, but this chapter should have revealed quite a lot about you: the way you see yourself, the way others see you and the way that you want to be. However, your replies to the questions and the way that you tackled the exercises are not set in stone. You may have changed your mind about certain things next week, or the week after. That doesn't matter too much, after all there is no right or wrong way to work through this chapter. It wasn't meant as homework, but an opportunity for you to learn more about yourself. With luck it will have achieved that.

CASE HISTORIES

Michelle shouldn't deceive herself

Michelle has always enjoyed wearing good clothes and priding herself on her fashion sense. So it's not surprising that a large part of any money she has goes on clothes. She always buys the trendiest and most modern garments she can lay her hands on, modelling herself as much as possible on what the 'stars' are wearing. She thinks that this makes her look very attractive, sophisticated and somehow more mature and adult. But her friends see things slightly differently. To them Michelle is pleasant enough to be around, but all she ever thinks about is clothes and she has no other interests to talk about. So instead of thinking of her as being adult, Michelle's friends tend to see her as pretty immature, as does every interviewer when she goes for her first job, dressed up rather like a pop singer.

Kevin shouldn't underestimate himself

Kevin has always thought of himself as being a rather 'run of the mill' character, who has never really done anything with his life or achieved anything and certainly with no real skills. But then he sat down and completed his own self assessment. What he found surprised him. On completing the questionnaire above he found that he really was quite creative, frequently coming up with new ideas when there was a problem at work to be solved. What surprised him even more was that his family and friends also thought of him as being creative. Many people tend to be just too modest about themselves and their achievements and it is only when they take a deeper look at themselves that they realise they are a better 'product' than they had first thought.

3
What is Your Market?

The previous chapter should have given you a good insight into your character and highlighted some of your strengths and weaknesses. This chapter looks at the other side of the coin by identifying and analysing what people and the job market want from you.

WHO DO YOU WANT TO MARKET TO?

As mentioned in chapter 1 there are many situations in which you might want to market yourself and this will involve many different types of people or groups. These can include work colleagues, your boss, friends and family, interviewers, customers and clients, staff, professional groups, even potential girlfriends or boyfriends. And each of them may require a different approach. You will also need to accept that you are unlikely to be able to market yourself equally to everybody because you won't either have the time to do this or because some groups will be mutually exclusive: you can't run with the fox and hunt with the hounds. If some groups are mutually exclusive—that is you can't influence both at the same time without seeming to be manipulative or scheming—you will need to set priorities and make choices.

Write down the three most important groups of people that you want to market yourself to now:

1 . . . .
2 . . . .
3 . . . .

Why do you want to market yourself to these particular groups?
Write your reasons here:

1 . . . .
2 . . . .
3 . . . .

WHAT DO MARKETS WANT?

Having identified those you want to influence, you now need to
find out what these people are actually looking for. To use an
extreme example, there would be no point in trying to market
yourself as a mature and responsible person who could be a
secretary for a firm of solicitors and then turning up for the job
interview in a clown suit! If you are applying for a job with an
accountant or a bank they will expect you to be trustworthy, good
with numbers, be able to pay attention to detail and to be
conservative in the way you dress. Therefore if you want to increase
your chances you will need to create a package of these things.
Likewise, if you want to convince a rock band that you can market
them, you (the product) will have to create an altogether different
marketing package.

Write down what your three chosen markets will expect from you
in the way you behave, the skills you have, the way you dress and
anything else that you can think is relevant:

1 . . . .
2 . . . .
3 . . . .

Are you able to give these markets what they want, or are there
some areas in which you don't meet the markets' needs? Where do
you fall down?

1 . . . .
2 . . . .
3 . . . .

WHAT SKILLS DO YOU HAVE?

Don't let your immediate reaction be 'what skills?' You have far more skills than you think and this is the place to really sing your own praises. To help you, think of a skill as being something that you have had to make an effort to learn. Riding a bike, learning to cook, swim, play cricket or climb a tree are all skills as much as learning a language, driving a car, or using a computer. The purpose of this section is to give you confidence that you have and can learn skills as much as identifying skills that will be useful in marketing yourself.

Write down 20 skills that you have:

1 . . . . 11 . . . .
2 . . . . 12 . . . .
3 . . . . 13 . . . .
4 . . . . 14 . . . .
5 . . . . 15 . . . .
6 . . . . 16 . . . .
7 . . . . 17 . . . .
8 . . . . 18 . . . .
9 . . . . 19 . . . .
10 . . . . 20 . . . .

Now write down another 20:

1 . . . . 11 . . . .
2 . . . . 12 . . . .
3 . . . . 13 . . . .
4 . . . . 14 . . . .
5 . . . . 15 . . . .
6 . . . . 16 . . . .
7 . . . . 17 . . . .
8 . . . . 18 . . . .
9 . . . . 19 . . . .
10 . . . . 20 . . . .

The skills that you have written down can largely be divided into 'general' skills, which are useful in a wide range of jobs and industries, and 'specific' skills which are special to a particular type of work. Write down those skills that you think might be useful in a job or career that you might want to follow:

1 . . . . 6 . . . .
2 . . . . 7 . . . .
3 . . . . 8 . . . .

WHAT SKILLS DO YOU NEED?

You may have skills, but are they ones that industry will be interested in? These are some of the general skills and attributes that you might have listed and which are of interest to a wide range of companies:

- Reliability
- Ability to get on with others
- Ability to manage others
- Ability to organise and manage yourself
- Confidence
- Communications skills
- Motivation
- Good work record
- Ability to take criticism
- Ability to work on your own
- Decision making skills.

In particular there are a number of skill areas which are especially valuable for anyone to have. In no particular order these are:

Driving skills
The car is the most versatile form of transport, and useful not only in getting you to and from work but also for your work. Indeed, there are some jobs, especially in sales and the like, where not being able to drive would prevent you from taking the job.

Computer skills
The computer is now a major business tool, and one that is increasingly forcing its way into the home. In the next ten years, knowing nothing about computers will put you at a serious disadvantage not only in the workplace, but also in life generally. As well as becoming familiar with how computers work and overcoming a fear of them, you should become skilled in the use of word-processors (programmes that turn a computer into an extremely powerful typewriter) and spreadsheets (these help you with accounts and to do cost projections).

Office technology and IT skills
As well as computers, the modern office is full of fax machines, printers, photocopiers, scanners and complicated telephone systems. Knowing how each works and how to use them while perhaps not giving your career an immense push forward will at least make life very much easier for you and create the impression that you are a competent person, well worth having on the team.

Keyboard skills
These go hand in hand with computer skills. Being fast, effective and error free at the computer or typewriter keyboard can take a lot of the mechanical drudgery out of the working day. It also means that you will not be reliant on others, secretaries or assistants, to type letters or reports for you. This is especially useful if you are working on confidential or private documents that you don't want others to see. If you don't have the keyboard skills and have to type a letter yourself you will waste valuable time and probably end up with a poor looking piece of work that doesn't impress.

Language skills
The UK's growing relationship with the outside world, particularly Europe, means that language skills are now in great demand. Don't delude yourself that so many people speak English that you don't need to make the effort. It may be true, but talking to someone in their own language will impress them and give you an advantage. It will also open up numerous career opportunities both in Britain and abroad.

People management skills
Whatever line of work you are in you will have to deal with others, so an ability to get on well with people will stand you in good stead. People management skills are particularly important when you have to supervise or manage the work of others to complete a project.

Professional qualifications
These aren't always an essential to getting on, but they increase your professionaliam and give you extra credibility. Only you can decide whether possessing a particular professional qualification will be worth all the time and effort of acquiring it.

Any new skill

Learning anything new is a worthwhile exercise because it helps keep your mind alive and open. So, if you don't need to learn anything at the moment, still learn something.

How many of these general and transportable skills do you have?

. . . .
. . . .
. . . .
. . . .

You can find out what skills and attributes a particular industry or company wants by:

● asking people who already work in that industry or company what skills are required

● reading books on the industry, particularly basic ones

● reading general management books by well-known entrepreneurs

● reading trade journals

● reading biographies of famous people in the industry

● talking to career advisers

● contacting the industry association and seeking their advice.

UPDATING YOUR SKILLS

Whatever your chosen career or type of work, you can't expect that the skills you will require will remain the same. You will have to be continually aware of changes within the industry that may need you to look at your skills to see if they are still appropriate. If they are not you will eventually either have to retrain yourself or move into another line of work.

So, whatever age you are, whatever your circumstances, you

should always be looking to update and add to your skills. This not only keeps you in the habit of learning something new (the mind takes a rest when it hasn't been asked to learn anything new for a while), but makes you a more flexible and rounded individual who can be asked to take on more testing tasks. Just as sports such as cricket have their all rounders who are particularly valuable players because they can both bowl and bat, so you are more valuable as an all rounder employee with wide ranging skills to call on.

Where to find help

There are a number of useful organisations around which can help you not only to improve your self-marketing, but also to learn new skills.

Job Clubs
Their leaders will help you look for jobs, prepare CVs and make applications. You must have been unemployed for a number of months before being eligible to attend. When you do attend you must do so regularly.

TAPS
Training Access Points provide a database of training and education opportunities and information on open learning.

PICKUP (Professional, Industrial and Commercial Updating)— this is a database that is mainly for people who are already in work.

ECCTIS (Educational Counselling and Credit Transfer Information Service)—this service offers a database of information on almost 80,000 courses in the UK.

Colleges of Further Education
Once called technical colleges, these offer qualifications that range from GCSEs and A levels to job specific training. Courses are full and part-time. These colleges are open to anyone over the age of 16. You can either use the qualifications you obtain here as an end in themselves or as a stepping stone to further qualifications.

Universities
These are learning establishments which offer degree courses which can provide the academic qualifications you need to form the foundations of a career.

Access courses
These are set up by colleges working in conjunction with a university, polytechnic or college of higher education for those who want a degree but don't have the standard entry requirements.

Open learning and distance learning
These are a development of a correspondence course. Students learn from course books, tutorials with course staff and by doing support assignments.

The Open University
Now a well established learning establishment, the OU lets you obtain qualifications in both academic and vocational courses.

The University of the Third Age
This organisation does not offer formal qualifications, but rather aims to involve older people in teaching and research, as well as encouraging them to learn by forming learning groups.

LEARNING SKILLS MORE EFFECTIVELY

You should always try to keep on learning and to improve your skills. For one thing the world is constantly changing with new techniques, ideas and information being made available all the time, and you need to keep abreast of them. Also, it is the height of arrogance (and stupidity) to think that you know all that you need to about yourself or a subject.

One reason why some people have this attitude is because they have tried self improvement courses, books and tapes and found that they didn't work. Sometimes this could be down to the poor quality and ineffectiveness of the materials they were using, but generally it can be put down to the persons themselves. So, if you are to succeed with any programme of self-improvement you should bear the following points in mind:

- First, concentrate on one area of self-improvement at a time. This will focus your efforts and stop you becoming confused. Therefore if you want to improve your public speaking, decision making abilities and general level of confidence, don't immediately enrol on courses or buy books and tapes on all three. Choose one area that you will tackle for the next three months, then move on to the other areas.

- Second, try and build up a whole stack of reasons why it would be worth your while to go on a typing or wordprocessing course or whatever. These reasons will give you the motivation you need to start and equally importantly to finish your self-improvement course. Make these reasons strong enough and you will be able to achieve anything. If you are only half interested or just 'think it would be nice' to be able to wordprocess you will lack the motivation to keep going to the end.

- Third, once you have undertaken a programme of self-improvement then make sure that you practise your skills. After going to all the effort of learning something new, many people immediately think that they don't need to bother any more. If your self-improvement efforts are to mean anything then you must put your skills into effect.

Who can help you?

Each of us knows lots and lots of people from all walks of life. These include our family and relatives, friends, workmates, people we were at school or college with, neighbours, ex-neighbours, people we do business with, people we buy things from, people we play sports with—the list goes on and on. However, few people think of all these people as assets in their self-marketing campaign.

Why assets? Because each of these people may have some invaluable experience, knowledge that we might be able to call upon. Some people might think this is being manipulative, a case of 'it's who you know' and not 'what you know'. Whether you take this view is up to you, but if you want to market yourself successfully it can be worthwhile using your contacts.

Try and write down at least 100. You may be able to double that number quite easily.

When you have finished, go through the list and for each name try and identify what you think their skills are, what knowledge they might have, who they might know. For some names on your list you won't need to spend much time on this. But for others you might have to spend extra time because of their range of interests and background.

Try and come up with a priority list of about 20 people whom it may be worth contacting because of their value to your self-marketing efforts. Now can you contact them without having to become a private detective? This may reduce the list by one third immediately, so that your list is now reduced to 12 to 14. Now rank these in order of importance to you, giving the number 1 to the person you are going to contact first.

But before you contact anyone you must think out your approach so that you don't offend or suggest that you are in any way exploiting them. Asking for the other person's help is a good way of winning them over, because it is always flattering to be asked for help. Be open with them, tell them that you want to get into the motor industry for instance, and ask them if they were in your position, how they would go about it. If you are lucky they may even offer to introduce you to someone who can help you. Never ask anyone directly for another person's name unless you know them particularly well.

And if anything comes of that person's help, drop them a letter and keep them posted even if you don't think they will be of any more help to you. This is only courteous and they still may be able to help you another time. If you can, repay them for their help and time in a more concrete way by doing a small favour for them.

CASE HISTORY

Jon adapts to change

Jon is a designer on magazines and a very good one at that. Since leaving art college 20 years ago he has used the skills he learned very successfully, making himself a good living as he moved from one magazine to another. But in recent years he has begun to find that magazines were wanting designers who knew how to design on computers, even if they weren't as experienced or as good as Jon. With each passing month it seemed to Jon that the situation was getting worse, with fewer and fewer publications wanting his undoubted skills. But Jon was now painted into a corner, he had to work full-time, so had no time to train up to a professional standard designing on a computer. In the end he had no choice. It was either train or go out of business. Jon borrowed £5,000 from the bank to cover his living expenses for a few months, bought an Apple Mac computer and learned how to design in modern hi-tech fashion. Jon's mistake had been in not paying enough attention to the trends in his own industry; he managed to make the change, but others aren't so lucky.

4
Marketing Yourself Through Confidence

No matter why you are trying to market yourself, one of the most basic skills that you need to possess is **confidence**. This is vitally important as it underpins everything else you might do. It is almost certainly the attribute that most of us would like to have in far greater quantities. Haven't we all at one time or another admired the person who is able to stand up and say their piece, to put their point of view across strongly, to talk confidently to literally anyone?

So, if you want to market yourself to your full potential, you must possess confidence to a reasonable degree, but even if you are a real shrinking violet, you can improve your self confidence.

WHAT IS CONFIDENCE?

In part, confidence is a result of the way in which we were brought up and taught by others to behave and believe. In part it is the way that we have learned to react to different situations.

Self-confidence means many different things to different people but really it is all about having faith in yourself. Very often when we lack confidence in ourselves it is because of what we believe others will think of us. We are sure that they will laugh at our actions, or complain about what we have done. If you don't have enough confidence in yourself then you will end up not doing some things because you consider the possible consequences too painful; these can be things that you want to do or have to do.

The problem of over confidence
Having sufficient self-confidence is one thing, but having it to an excessive degree can be a problem if it makes you feel you can do

anything, even when you don't possess the skills or the abilities to do it well. Over confidence then leads to failure.

Checklist—How confident are you?

You probably have a good idea of your own level of self confidence, but it is worth running through this checklist just to confirm your assessment.

Do you feel you have confidence in yourself?   Yes/No

Do you have a bit of an ego and like showing off
to others?   Yes/No

Do you like telling jokes and stories to a group of
friends or even strangers?   Yes/No

Have you ever been on the stage in front of an
audience?   Yes/No

Do you talk a lot in front of others, telling everyone
your opinions and what you think?   Yes/No

Are you able to go ahead and do something even though
everyone else says that you are wrong?   Yes/No

Are you able to do things by yourself or do you need
the moral support of others before you go ahead?   Yes/No

Can you chat quite happily and flirt with members
of the opposite sex?   Yes/No

Do you think of a problem as being a new challenge to
overcome?   Yes/No

If someone asks you to do something you have never
done before do you see this as a challenge that is worth
having a go at?   Yes/No

If someone asks you to try out something new is your
immediate reaction normally to say 'yes'?   Yes/No

Write down five times in the last year when you have lacked confidence:

1 . . . .
2 . . . .
3 . . . .
4 . . . .
5 . . . .

Try and remember what it was like when you felt a great lack of
confidence. How did you stand then? What tone or strength did
your voice have? How did your body feel generally? Try and feel
a lack of confidence right now. How does your body feel and look
(check yourself in a mirror)?

Write down five times in the last year when you have felt
particularly confident:

1 . . . .
2 . . . .
3 . . . .
4 . . . .
5 . . . .

Try and remember what it was like when you were feeling
confident. How did you stand? What tone or strength did your
voice have? How did your body feel generally? Think of something
now about which you feel confident. Does your body feel different
now? In what way?

BUILDING YOUR CONFIDENCE

So how do you go about making yourself appear more confident,
even when you don't feel it? Well, there are a number of ways.
These are some of the most common techniques.

Mental attitude

Having self-confidence is very much a question of mental attitude.
If you think that you can do something then you are far better
equipped to achieve it than someone who only tackles the task half
heartedly because they aren't certain of themselves. And you can
'think' yourself into a more confident frame of mind, even if you

are something of an introvert. Above all you must remember that you **can** become more confident. Everyone feels nervous from time to time, even people such as politicians when under the television spotlight or centre stage. The difference is that they have learned to control their nerves so well that their nervousness does not show. So right now, begin by thinking more positively. This is largely a question of habit so the more you do of it, the better you will become.

Find a role model

Identify someone you know who has a lot of self-confidence and begin copying what they do. Ideally this should be someone that you come into contact regularly in your life. It could be a work colleague, your boss, a friend or a member of the family. Begin studying them and try to find out what makes them tick. When they are being confident how do they behave, how do they stand and walk, how do they speak, what do they say and when do they say it? Do they do anything in particular to psych themselves up such as a ritual or a certain way of doing things?

If you can't find someone in real life to model yourself on, then you should be able to find someone on the television and this does have its advantages. First, you can look at them very closely and even record their movements so that you can look time and time again at what they do and the way they do it. This gives you a great opportunity to study the way that they move, their mannerisms, their gestures and their postures. However, it does mean that you see them generally in only one particular environment, the television studio. Particularly when watching people on the television have a note pad and pen with you to write down your thoughts.

Whatever you do, become as good as you can be at it because the better you are at doing something the more confident you become. Let's take something very simple: for instance, if you drive, especially if you have been driving for some time, you are confident about your own abilities. You don't 'think' about when to press the pedals or turn the steering wheel, but do it automatically as and when you need to. Contrast this with the way you were when you began learning to drive. Think of how nervous you were then! Being certain that you can do the job is a great confidence builder.

Even if you are short, always try to walk tall, with your shoulders back and chest out. People who walk around with their shoulders slouched give the impression that they are uncertain, lack confidence and have a weak personality.

Look for professional help

If you would like help in building your confidence then it may be worth seeking the help of professionals. There are several ways in which you do this. You might want to book yourself on an assertiveness course at your local education college, or even pay for a course of hypnotherapy, which has proved of benefit to some people who lack self-confidence. However, if you do use hypnotherapy then you should always make sure that the therapist is well qualified and runs a reputable practice. And be warned, this can be a quite expensive method of overcoming your lack of confidence.

You're already a success

Presumably you think there is some point in marketing yourself, otherwise you wouldn't be reading this book now. But just to give yourself a little ego boost, think of all the successes that you have had over the years. It doesn't matter how big or small they have been, just think. And before you say that you have always been a loser and never achieved anything, stop. You have. What about winning a form prize, scoring a winning goal at hockey, passing your driving test, raising funds for charity, bringing up a child. Our worlds are full of our successes and yet for the most part we fail to recognise what we have achieved.

List the successes, no matter how small, that you have had in your life:

. . . .
. . . .
. . . .
. . . .
. . . .
. . . .

ROLE PLAYING

One of the very best ways of building up your confidence to deal with a wide variety of situations is to practise role play. You will need someone to help you to do this, preferably someone who is willing to put in the time and to take this seriously.

Role playing is esentially a dress rehearsal for any new situation that you are liable to encounter. This could be a job interview, a business presentation or meeting many new people for the first time.

At its simplest it involves you playing yourself while the other person acts out the part of the interviewer, client, boss or stranger. The idea is to create as realistically as possible the situation that you are going to meet, which will give you practice at dealing with that situation and take the 'newness' away from it when you meet the real thing. You should therefore make your role playing as effective as possible by trying to simulate the conditions in which it will take place and wearing the appropriate clothes. You will need to brief the other person about what it is you want them to say and talk about.

When you first start role playing take things easy and just get used to the idea, but then begin making things progressively harder, with the other person asking you awkward questions, generally putting you on the spot and trying to unnerve you.

Role play for as long and as often as you think necessary, swapping roles if appropriate to give yourself a rest from one character and to get another perspective on the situation. And remember, if you want to get the most out of role play you should make it as realistic as possible.

PRACTISING OTHER SELF-CONFIDENCE SKILLS

As you become more self-confident you should take every opportunity to practise your newly acquired skill. If you don't do this then you will find your skill level falls off and the time that you have spent learning to become more confident will be wasted.

One way to ensure this doesn't happen is to set yourself **targets** and goals to achieve each day or each week, which test your self-confidence to different degrees. These can range from activities that give the mildest of butterfly attacks, to those that almost scare the hell out of you. These are some of the activities you could set yourself to do:

● Make a fuss in a restaurant or café if your food isn't right

- Wear something that's garish in colour, if you wouldn't do this normally

- Buy a 'girlie' or gay magazine, if you wouldn't do this normally

- Buy condoms at a busy chemist's counter, if you wouldn't do this normally

- Talk to a total stranger in a lift

- Talk to a stranger in a crowded room

- Stand up and speak in a public meeting

- Introduce yourself to someone new.

There are many other activities that you could choose to test yourself. Write down 10 such activities that will test your self-confidence. These should be a mixture of relatively easy and hard activities.

1 . . . .
2 . . . .
3 . . . .
4 . . . .
5 . . . .
6 . . . .
7 . . . .
8 . . . .
9 . . . .
10 . . . .

USING POSITIVE PEOPLE

Each one of us tends to feed emotionally off the people that we find around us. For instance, if your friends are sad they can 'bring you down'. On the other hand if they are happy then you can be pulled up with them even if you were miserable beforehand. The trouble is that, while each of us will at one time feel up or down, there are some people in this world who are permanently on a downer.

Now, one of the biggest destroyers of any confidence you may have is the moaning minnie who is constantly negative, belittling what you are trying to achieve and telling you that you can never succeed. Those people you can do without.

On the other hand it does make sense to surround yourself with positive people, those who tell you that you **can** do something and that you are able to succeed. Why? Because of course their attitude will rub off on you. You will start being as enthusiastic about things as they are, you will start looking forward rather than back. These 'positives' can come from every walk of life. Look for them.

List as many people with a positive outlook on life as you can:

. . . .
. . . .
. . . .
. . . .

Write down the occasions and places where you can meet and be with them regularly:

. . . .
. . . .
. . . .
. . . .

On the other hand you will want to avoid the negative people in life, because they bring you down with their constant whining that there is never anything good about their lives. Write the names of the Mr and Mrs Negatives that you know:

. . . .
. . . .
. . . .
. . . .

List the places where you come across these people:

. . . .
. . . .
. . . .
. . . .

DEVELOPING A POSITIVE MENTAL ATTITUDE

When marketing yourself it is very important that you have a strongly positive mental attitude. This does wonders for your confidence.

However, after years of being negative about yourself and your way of life, you may find it difficult to begin thinking positively. If that's the case, there are a number of techniques you can try to improve matters.

- Tackle only one small area of your life at a time, for instance by being more positive in just your family life for the time being. When you have got into the habit of doing this, progress to your work or social life. Keep going even if you fail at first.

- When you find yourself saying no to a request or a suggestion, stop and ask yourself whether you are doing this out of habit, rather than making the right decision.

- Get yourself into the habit of being positive by making small positive decisions. These can be about anything as long as they are in the affirmative and you make them quickly. The more you do this the more of a habit it will become.

- Whenever you think of something negative try and see also something positive about the situation. For example, if your car breaks down and has to go into the garage for repairs think of this as an opportunity to get fit, or to learn more about cars so that you can undertake the repairs next time.

- Think of the 'negativisms' that you use in your daily life. These may include such phrases such as 'that looks hard', 'I wonder if I can do that?', 'I'm not sure about this'.

Write down the negativisms that you use in your everyday life.

. . . .
. . . .
. . . .

Now make yourself a promise that you will do your best to eradicate these expressions from your personal vocabulary.

BECOMING CALMER

Generally when you are confident you are calm, but the reverse is also true. So, by staying calm even when you are under stress and pressure you will tend to feel more confident. There are many relaxation techniques around and it is worth while learning at least one method. Whichever you choose, the important things to learn are how to relax your neck and jaw muscles as this will not only help calm your nerves but make you look less tense to others, and to breathe deeply. You should remember that taking a deep breath in is only half the story. While this fills the lungs and body with oxygen, you will need to get rid of the carbon dioxide you build up by exhaling deeply. A build up of carbon dioxide in the blood is one of the physiological causes of nervousness and anxiety.

MAKING LONG-TERM BEHAVIOUR CHANGES

Building up your confidence is just one of the changes that you can make to your behaviour. But making the effort and taking the time to change our behaviour is no good if after a few days, weeks or months we go back to our old ways. Below is a technique that should help you make those behavioural changes stick, whether you want to make yourself more confident or improve yourself in some other way. If the technique seems rather strange and unfamiliar, stay with it. It does work and is just one of the many techniques that you can profitably use from the fascinating world of Neuro Linguistic Programming (NLP). For anyone who is serious about changing particular behaviours and habits then NLP can provide you with some extremely powerful methods for doing so. Several books on the subject are recommended in the Useful Information section at the back of this book.

Step 1

Imagine the behaviour you want to change. See yourself as if on television exhibiting the behaviour. For your self-marketing purposes this could be an interview with a prospective employer, or a meeting you are having with an important client. Watch in your mind's eye what happens as the interview progresses. Consciously note the things that you do well and the things that you do less well, the bits of behaviour that seem to be working for you and the ones that don't. Watch carefully.

Step 2

Now think of all the bits that were bad about what you have just seen and think about what better bits of behaviour you could put in their place.

Step 3

When you have done this, run through the scene again, but this time replace the bad things you did with the good things you have just thought of. You may find this difficult to do at first but keep at it, it will get easier. If you find that you are going back to the first set of behaviours or different ones entirely, stop, and start again.

Step 4

When you are comfortable doing this, imagine that you are now not watching yourself on television but the actual actor playing the part of you. You feel what they do, behave the way they do and talk like they do. Do your very best to experience just what it is they are experiencing. Act out the scene in your head. The more intensely you can do this the better, but make sure that you are still doing the right behaviours and not falling back into the old ways. Again, if you find that you are going back to the first set of behaviours, stop and start anew.

CASE HISTORIES

Malcolm shuns the limelight

Malcolm has had problems with his confidence from his childhood, when he was small for his age and continually being bullied by others. And though bright in many ways, Malcolm knows that he misses out on a lot of chances because he doesn't push himself. If he goes out to a pub he blushes and stutters if ever he is the centre of attention or asked to tell a joke or story. He has missed out on countless job opportunities and promotions simply because he is seen as a shrinking violet who has little to contribute. The unfortunate thing is that Malcolm is probably the best at the job in his department. In situations like these a lack of self-confidence is crippling and can really ruin someone's life. Unless Malcolm decides that he is going to change his ways he will be stuck in a rut of mediocrity, dreaming of what might have been for the rest of his life!

Marie prepares herself

Before she goes into an important meeting, makes a vital telephone call or attends an interview, Marie does her very best to psych herself, much as a sports player will do before going out on court or the pitch. Though there are different techniques for doing this, such as shouting, going for a run or some other brisk physical exercise, Marie finds that the most practical approach for her is to listen to some inspiring music before making the call. She likes stirring classical music best, though that's just her personal preference. At the end of her favourite piece she turns off her Walkman, or switches off her car cassette if she is travelling to a meeting, and full of confidence and energy is ready to do battle.

5
Creating the Right Image

WHAT IS IMAGE?

Your image is the overall picture you present to the world. Image is determined by a large number of factors including the way you look physically, how you dress and speak, and the manner in which you walk and behave. Consequently everyone has a different image.

In many cases we have several images with each one being on show to a different group or type of people. For example, a man who is considered a cold blooded and ruthless businessman in his working life may be thought of as a loving husband by his wife, a wonderful father by his children, a generous individual by the community and just a little boy by his own mother. There is nothing wrong with having several images for yourself.

WHAT'S YOUR IMAGE?

Your current image may be wholly acceptable for what you want to achieve (improbable, but highly fortunate), or it may be totally wrong or unacceptable. Most probably your image will be somewhere between the two. You will wish to change certain aspects of it, while leaving other parts alone. The earlier self-assessment chapter should already have given an indication about how others see you.

Before you can really begin to make any sort of changes, you must know and decide the new image that you want. What this will be is largely dependent upon who you want to influence.

WHO TO INFLUENCE?

Write down the names of five groups of people or, better still, individuals whom you would like to influence positively:

1 . . . .
2 . . . .
3 . . . .
4 . . . .
5 . . . .

To make sure that these are the right people to influence, write down your reasons for influencing them in particular here:

1 . . . .
2 . . . .
3 . . . .
4 . . . .
5 . . . .

What aspects of character, behaviour and appearance do you think they will be positively influenced by? You should be able to obtain a good idea of this by their past behaviour, if you know them; or by the general requirements and demands of the industry, if you don't. For instance, undertakers, no matter how funny they may be in private, are expected to have a serious demeanour when at work; bank managers are expected to dress soberly and look at problems seriously; while advertising copywriters who are creative are expected to be similarly creative in the way that they behave and dress. Write down those aspects of character, behaviour and appearance that will positively affect the people you want to influence:

1 . . . .
2 . . . .
3 . . . .
4 . . . .
5 . . . .

Write down the aspects of character, behaviour and appearance that will negatively affect the people you want to influence and will therefore make them think less of you:

1 . . . .
2 . . . .

3 . . . .
4 . . . .
5 . . . .

Now, choose **one** of the groups or individuals that you want to influence. Go through the positive aspects of character, behaviour and appearance that they want and expect from you. Decide if you have them already or not. If you don't possess these particular characteristics are you willing or able to acquire them? Write your answers down here:

. . . .

. . . .

Complete the exercise above for the negative aspects of your nature. Do you possess them or not? Again, write your answers down here:

. . . .

. . . .

CHOOSING AN IMAGE

You shouldn't try and change your image too much too soon. If you try for too dramatic a change this will look incredibly false to those who already know you; without a lot of effort you won't be able to keep it up in front of those who don't know you; and you will start feeling uncomfortable and lacking in confidence virtually immediately.

Rather, the image you want should be an extension of the type of person you are now. If you do think you need to make a radical change in your image then think about doing this in stages by changing just one element of your appearance or general image at a time, such as the way you dress, or the way you speak, or the way you behave, not all three at once.

As you have seen, you can have different images for different people or groups of people. For example, if your customers are generally young you may want to dress in a more relaxed way so that they feel you are part of their group. But dressing in the same way wouldn't be sensible if you were having a meeting with the bank manager when a more formal approach would be better. However, dress differently from others if you want to set yourself apart from them and to appear more dynamic.

Creating an image through clothes

When you are in business or at work it is important to wear clothes that are right for the job and for the occasion. It would be appropriate to wear overalls when working in a workshop, but inappropriate to see the bank manager in them.

Smart clothes can be particularly important if you are involved in a service business, especially one in which you need to inspire in others the confidence that you can do the right job.

Creating the right image for the office

When choosing your business clothes you should not be too fashion conscious, but aim rather for styles that are classics. If you aren't quite sure what these styles are like, take a walk along the streets at rush hour and see what business people are wearing. Also start looking through fashion and lifestyle magazines. There are also a number of books on better dressing so start reading these.

Now with some ideas in your head, wander around clothes shops and begin creating new wardrobes and styles in your head. When you finally come to buy, choose a few quality clothes that will keep their shape and look good rather than going for a lot of cheaper clothes that lose their shape quickly and become tatty. The better the look of your clothes the more confident you will feel.

If you want to add some character to your business clothes then you can always do so by choosing shirts that have different coloured collars, interesting ties and cuff links, or attractive brooches or earrings.

Suits

Suits are frequently seen as being 'standard' wear for the office. Single breasted suits make you seem more approachable than double breasted. You come across as being more relaxed especially when you wear the jacket open. There is no need to invest in a pin stripe unless you want your image to be rather old fashioned and stolid. Even in the traditional City professions, pinstripes are losing favour.

Jackets and trousers

These are an alternative to suits, and a cost effective one at that because you can mix and match them, which you can't do with suits.

Skirts and blouses

Opt again for classical styles, longer rather than short and subtle rather than loud. Bright colours may make you stand out but they can create entirely the wrong image, branding you as a 'power dresser'—not always the best way to be seen if you are in quite a low level job or have a boss who is nervous of you and your attempts to climb up the career ladder. Above all, try to avoid the flirtatious, sexy look. Even if you feel completely comfortable with this you can get yourself in trouble with the office wolf and with other women who feel threatened or overshadowed by you.

Ties

For job interviews go for a rather understated classically patterned silk tie. This looks smart, creates a good impression and suggests that you want to be taken seriously. Personnel officers are said to subconsciously favour ties that have an element of blue in them. Whatever type of tie you choose avoid ones that are too wide or too narrow.

Shoes

Make sure that you have two pairs of shoes at least; then you have a spare pair to wear if one pair needs repairing. Always keep shoes well repaired (you don't want to look down at heel) and when they begin to show signs of wear then take them along to the cobblers. Clean and polish your shoes when you take them off. Warm leather absorbs polish better and therefore achieves a better shine than cold leather. If you don't want the uppers to crease then put them on shoe trees, which will keep the leather stretched.

Accessories

A good quality watch looks attractive and does make an impression, but there is no need to go overboard by buying the most expensive around. A good leather strap can help transform an otherwise dull and even cheap timepiece. Black is the obvious strap colour, though a strong rich brown one can offer a distinctive contrast, especially when worn with a dark suit. Don't go for straps that are peculiar or unusual as they are frequently inelegant or just look downright odd. Above all, avoid watches that emit regular bleeps on the hour, or chime 'Jingle Bells' at the touch of a button. Even if you never use the facilities they will always go off at least once or twice unexpectedly and at the most inappropriate of times. Noisy watches only serve to distract and annoy others and that's not good if you want to be seen as mature and responsible.

If you are going to carry a briefcase make sure that you buy a good quality one. Cheap briefcases downgrade an otherwise professional image instantly. Those creating the best impression are leather, stylish and slim. Large cases don't create a good image. Always keep them clean and well polished.

Hair
Your hair can say a great deal about you, and if it's not right then it will definitely be saying the wrong things. Hair should always be well cut and kept well groomed. You should avoid extremes in style and colour if you want to be taken seriously and to create a good impression.

Glasses
If you need glasses then do experiment to find the frames that best suit your face. Try wearing contact lenses as a better alternative as they help 'open' up your face and make you more accessible.

KEEPING UP YOUR IMAGE

After you have bought them, make sure that your clothes are always clean, pressed and well looked after. Hang your clothes up after wearing them so they stay uncreased. This is also good discipline, so do it no matter how tired you are at the end of a day.

If you have any running repairs to do on your outfits—buttons to be sewn on, hems stitched up, stains removed—then do this when you take the clothes off. If you don't, and hang them up or put them away, then inevitably you will re-discover the problem only when you come to put them on again, and probably when you don't have the time to remedy matters. If you are simply too tired to mend or repair clothes when you take them off, then at least make a large and very distinctive note to yourself to take care of them at the first opportunity.

Changing image on a low budget
You don't need to go out and buy a whole new wardrobe of clothes to make a new image for yourself (though sometimes that may be

the only solution if you are making a radical change in your image); thankfully you can do quite a lot without breaking the bank.

Even if your clothes aren't top of the range, or even that good a quality, you should always make sure that they are clean and well ironed or pressed. Anything else will look scruffy.

You can do much by paying closer attention to accessories, which cost a lot less than a new suit or jacket. A range of good quality ties, cufflinks, earrings or necklaces when used with your usual outfit can give it a lift. However, don't fall into the trap of over accessorising or being too flashy. Especially when you are trying to create a professional or businesslike image, less is more.

Always try and keep one suit, jacket, skirt or trousers for 'best', which you can wear for more important occasions.

If your budget is tight but you still want to look well groomed, then go to hairdressers or hairdressing colleges who are frequently on the look out for 'models' on which their students and trainees can practise. Don't worry. You won't end up scalped as the trainees will be fully supervised.

You can even keep an eye out for some good quality secondhand clothes and suits. These will do as a stop gap as long as they are dry cleaned and well pressed. Many of the clothes in Oxfam and nearly new shops are of surprisingly good quality, and often little used.

Feeling comfortable

If you are making an important presentation, having a job interview or particularly want to impress then be sure that you are comfortable in what you are wearing. You may have bought something very new and very expensive, but if you feel awkward when wearing it this will show in your mannerisms, voice and whole behaviour.

So, when you have bought something new, wear it around the house for an hour or two, before venturing out to an important meeting. This will give you time to 'iron out' any of its bugs, such as loose threads, sewn up jacket pockets or hems coming down. Wear new shoes around for a while if they have leather soles as this will take some of the slipperiness away. The last thing you want is to be falling over the minute you get onto the shiny floor of an office.

YOUR OTHER IMAGES

Remember that image is not just something that is confined to your work environment. You have an image even when you are relaxing in the pub, going out to dinner with friends or playing football. And the image that you have in one element of your life can contradict what you are trying to achieve in other areas. For instance, if you dress immaculately and maturely at work your boss might be surprised and perhaps a little bit worried if he bumped into you in a restaurant when you were rolling drunk, dressed in torn jeans and rude t-shirt and threatening to fight anyone you could lay your hands on!

What about your car?

Old bangers are great for getting around. And because your friends are probably no better off than yourself, the look, make and model of your car doesn't matter at all to them. However, if you are after a particular job where image is important then turning up in an old wreck can be a positive disadvantage. So, if you don't have a good car, and don't have the cash to buy another one, what can you do? Quite bluntly the answer is don't make the failings of your car obvious.

Especially if it is an old banger make sure that your car is regularly serviced so there is less chance of it going wrong. If you don't, Murphy's Law will dictate that it won't start on the very morning you have a job interview or meeting.

Join a reputable breakdown and recovery organisation such as the AA, RAC or National Breakdown. This will give you more confidence on long trips. Take the Home Start option if your car is an older and less reliable model or make.

If your car is prone to breaking down try to make some prior arrangement with family, friends or neighbours to borrow their car in case you have a problem.

When you have a meeting don't try starting your car when ready to leave, but start it ten or 15 minutes beforehand; this will at least give you some extra time if you have a problem should overnight cold or bad weather have affected it.

Always leave for a meeting in plenty of time. If you have a problem on the way then at least there is a chance you will have some opportunity to recover from it.

If you do have an old banger then don't park it in the client's car park where he or anyone else in the company can see it. If you do have to park in the client's car park then put the car out of direct line of sight of the windows. You don't want your client to see you getting in or out of it.

And if your car is a little on the ancient and decrepit side, then don't bring up the subject of cars in an interview or meeting. Inevitably you will be asked what you drive and that could lead to embarrassment.

PREPARING FOR A MEETING OR INTERVIEW

Interviews and meetings can be make or break opportunities for you, so it is best to do some basic preparatory work to ensure that you create the right impression.

- As far as humanly possible you should always be prepared for a meeting, so do all the things that you have to do for it, well before time. The Boy Scouts' motto is 'Be Prepared'—it should also be yours.

- Always dress appropriately for the meeting. If you are wearing out-of-place clothes you will create the wrong impression and probably make yourself uncomfortable and uneasy in the process, just when you want to be confident.

- Be on time for the meeting.

- It goes without saying that you should always check that all zips and flies are firmly done up. Ties should also be well knotted, not too tightly, and done up to the top button, which should be buttoned. Ties should also be clean.

- Shirts and blouses should be buttoned up. It does not make a good impression if during a meeting you sit there showing off your hairy chest or your Wonderbra.

- Bad breath is an unpleasant experience for anyone on the receiving end, so make sure yours doesn't give offence by using breath freshening sweets just before going into a meeting or interview. And don't think that just because you don't have bad breath on one day, you won't suffer from it on another, since we are all affected by spicy food and our general state of health. If you suffer from bad breath on a regular basis then it is worth paying a visit to the doctor and also to the dentist as dental decay can create bad breath.

- Body odour can be an invisible assassin of ambitions by distracting others and generally making life unpleasant for all around. Make sure you don't become a BO victim by showering or bathing frequently and by using a good anti-perspirant and deodorant.

- Perfume and aftershave can make you feel good, but be sure you don't overdo the effect and that the quality of product is good. A rank, rancid and overpowering perfume or aftershave splashed all over you is a headstrong combination that others may find nauseating rather than refreshing, so always err on the side of caution.

- Shoes should be clean and laced up.

- Make sure that your face is clean and unmarked with no smudged make up to spoil the effect. Shave in plenty of time before going to a meeting or before you put on a clean shirt. If you don't, and cut yourself, then you will be faced with the prospect of a bloody collar or bits of tissue stuck all over your face—not the most attractive way to present yourself.

Creating a good first impression

When people see you for the first time they immediately draw conclusions about you. They 'do judge a book by its cover', therefore it is absolutely vital to make a good first impression when you are trying to market yourself. It may be a truism, but the saying 'you don't have a second chance to make a good first impression' is absolutely correct.

So, if you mess things up the first time round it will consequently be harder for you to recover the situation, whether it is in the next few minutes or at a later date.

- Wear the best clothes that you can.

- Don't be too flashy in what you wear. Again classic understatedness is the key. If you are in an area where you can exhibit a degree of creativeness then go ahead, but don't overdo it.

- Make sure your jacket, trouser or suit pockets aren't full of rubbish which you could inadvertently pull out during an important interview. In any case you should carry very little in your pockets because this will spoil the line of your clothes and diminish the overall look of what you are wearing. If you keep a handkerchief in your pocket, be certain that it is spotlessly clean and preferably of a single colour and not some garish combination of fluorescents.

- Again, make sure that hair is cut and groomed, shoes are clean and polished, shirt collar is sitting tidily and that tie is properly knotted.

- If you are really fidgety and full of nervous energy then take a brisk walk around the block to burn off some of the adrenalin, but don't leave this so late that you miss the start time of the appointment or arrive hot and flustered.

- Always be on time. Only when you are in a position of power can you be late for an appointment without it diminishing what you hope to achieve. If you are late it means one of three things: you are so poorly organised that you can't arrive for a meeting on time; or that you don't take the meeting seriously; or that you are just discourteous, simply not bothering to turn up on time. Always try to be on time. You only have to notice how people always look at a latecomer to see how serious this is.

- Don't take your coat in with you. Leave it at reception. Taking a coat into a meeting means that you will have to struggle to take it off if you wear it in, or spoil the cut, look and impression you create with your clothes if you carry it in over your arm. Either way you will always have to find somewhere to put your coat.

- When you enter a room for a meeting, have your jacket buttoned up, so that you look professional, tidy and businesslike. You can unbutton the jacket as the meeting progresses and everyone becomes more relaxed. For best effect you should unbutton your jacket after the most senior person in the room has unbuttoned theirs.

- When you are introduced to someone, pay careful attention to their name. This is precious and important to everybody, so knowing and using a person's name is a powerful tool. It makes them feel important, but they are also very protective about it and don't like you to get it wrong. If you don't pick up on the name in the first place, then ask the person to repeat their name, spelling it if necessary. And once you know their name repeat it several times yourself so that it becomes imprinted on your memory. When you get the opportunity write down their name and any details you can recall about them. When you meet them next and show that you know their pet poodle is called 'Rambo' they will be impressed.

- Shake hands when you introduce yourself and achieve some degree of eye contact with the other person.

- Start your conversation on a positive note. The last thing that anyone wants to hear from you in answer to the question, 'How are you?' is your heart-rending tale of an impending divorce or a catalogue of gruesome symptoms of ill-health that are best left to the privacy of the doctor's surgery. A bright smile, though not of the Cheshire Cat variety, gets you off to a good start.

- If you want to make an impact at an interview, go in with a list of questions to ask and points to raise, attached to a clip board. This shows that you are in the driving seat as much as the interviewer. After all you are making a career choice as much as they are choosing an employee.

Looking good in a meeting

During the meeting or interview sit upright and alert in your chair. If you sit forward you will look as though you are showing extra interest in the other person and what they are talking about. If you slouch in your chair you will look far too relaxed, laid back and inattentive almost to the point of discourtesy.

Try not to let your gaze wander from the speaker and out of a window or onto someone or something else in the room unless it is referred to in the conversation. Try to keep your eyes on the other person. However, the idea is not to try and stare them out so you don't need to hold them with the gaze of an eagle continually. Shift your eyes away from theirs slightly so that you are looking at a spot in the centre of their forehead just above the eyebrows.

Don't turn away from the other person when you are talking to them, make sure you are turned towards them.

Solve the problem of not knowing what to do with your hands by keeping them lightly folded on your lap. You can use them occasionally to make a point. Don't fold your arms, or cross your legs as you will look uncomfortable and as if you are trying to hide something—remember what was said about bad body language.

Don't keep your face deadpan, scowl or frown and if it seems the right thing to do even use humour. A smile or a laugh is a great way of breaking the ice and relieving tension.

Create a good impression after a meeting

Sending a quick letter to someone after you have met or been interviewed by them is an unusual courtesy that makes you more memorable. It also gives you the opportunity to emphasise a few of the points that were covered in your conversation. These letters can be used whether the meeting or interview has gone well or badly. A letter sent after a good meeting could go something like the one shown in Figure 1.

With this letter it doesn't matter that you may have made these

---

Dear Mrs Smith

I enjoyed meeting with you today and seeing your company first hand. You certainly made me quite at home and I know I would feel comfortable working for you. I am a little concerned however that I may not have emphasised a couple of points about my experience strongly enough.

First, . . .

Fig. 1. A simple courtesy letter.

Dear Mrs Smith

Thank you for meeting with me today. I much appreciated your
time. But I felt that I didn't do myself justice, for one reason or
another, and that you may well feel that I am an unsuitable person
for the position, because I didn't stress strongly enough a number
of points which I believe are in my favour.

First, . . .

Fig. 2. A letter sent after a bad meeting or interview.

sales points excellently at the interview, what you are doing is
emphasising them once again to the interviewer so that you are
remembered even more favourably. You can use the same technique when you have had a bad interview or meeting, though the
letter would be slightly different. See Figure 2.

If an interview has gone badly then a letter like this may help
you regain some lost ground. However, you must send it quickly
(first class post and on the same day of the interview) if it is to
stand any chance of success.

Travelling to meetings and interviews

It is amazing how many people make problems for themselves
when attending meetings and interviews, with the result that
they make a poor impression on the person they are going to
meet. However, a few simple precautions can remove many of the
potential difficulties:

- Before leaving home check that you have everything you need
  with you.

- Make sure that you are looking your best by being shipshape
  and Bristol fashion well beforehand. Iron clothes and polish
  shoes the night before. Don't leave it to the morning of a
  meeting when the unexpected may already be eating into your
  spare time.

- Assume that everything you need to do will take at least one third longer than you expect when you have to go to a meeting. Expect the unexpected to happen and allow for it.

- Know where you are going. Have to hand a photocopied map of the route with your destination marked. When you make arrangements for the meeting ask for exact directions for reaching the office and details of parking, if you are driving by car. It may be that there is a company car park which is always pretty empty. If not, then you might be forced to park in the street and that could involve you in a walk back.

- Always leave yourself plenty of time for things to go wrong *en route*. By building a safety margin into your travelling time you shouldn't arrive hot and flustered at your destination.

- If you have several meetings scheduled for the same day, then don't try to be too efficient by arranging them close together in the mistaken belief that you will save yourself time. Do leave enough time to journey between the two meetings and for the first meeting to over-run. If you have left enough time over then you will be less worried about running late and therefore still be able to give your full attention to the current meeting.

Developing your handshake

One important element of meeting someone for the first time is the impression that you give when you shake hands. This is important, because it is the first physical contact someone else has with you. A handshake should be firm and friendly with a reasonable amount of pressure. There is no room in this world for people, particularly men, who try and crush every bone in your hand. This impresses no one. It suggests that they either don't know their own strength, enjoy hurting people, or more likely have the mistaken belief that they are achieving some psychological mastery over you by their 'threatening' handshake.

If you know that you are due to shake hands with someone, then try to ensure your hand is warm and dry. If you suffer from sweaty hands then try to wipe off some of the sweat on a handkerchief hidden away in a jacket or trouser pocket. Don't take the handkerchief out to do this. Likewise if you suffer from cold hands and fingers try and warm them up before handshaking.

CHOOSING A ROLE MODEL

One of the very best ways of changing your image is to choose someone who can be a role model, someone whose style you can copy. You can even have several role models if you want and they don't have to be from the business world or from your particular industry, they could be sports people, politicians or actors. They just need to have a characteristic that you want to copy. For instance, you might choose to copy Richard Branson for his flair, or Roger Moore (as James Bond) for his confidence.

Decide on someone who will be your role model. Write their name here: . . . .

Why have you chosen them to be your role model?

. . . .
. . . .
. . . .
. . . .

How will you go about studying them? Will you see them often enough in order to be able to study them properly?

. . . .
. . . .

Checklist

Do you generally take pride in the way you look?	Yes/No
Have you polished your shoes today?	Yes/No
Have you already booked your next hair cut?	Yes/No
Have you had your suits and jackets dry cleaned in the last two months?	Yes/No
Have you had a shave today?	Yes/No
Have you put on perfume or aftershave today?	Yes/No

Action plan

1. Make a list of the main changes that you want to make to yourself, both big and small. If you are making a large change in your image then do this in stages. Decide what these stages are going to be and set a date for starting work on each one.

2. Commit yourself to trying to make at least one little improvement every week.

3. If your hair is not cut in the appropriate style then book yourself in for a hairdressing appointment now. Have the best cut you can afford.

4. If your clothes aren't right then you will need to buy new ones. Write down the date you will start shopping for them.

5. Read any books you can find on developing confidence. Give all the ideas a go, but don't be frightened of settling on just one or two ideas that you are comfortable with and seem to work for you.

6. Learn relaxation skills.

CASE HISTORIES

Mary becomes self-aware

Mary works for a public relations agency in the City of London. She enjoys the job but feels that she isn't progressing through the company's ranks as quickly as she would like and thinks that there may be something wrong with the image that she is creating of herself. She works through the assessment exercises above and comes up with a few conclusions. She decides that she needs to impress not just her immediate boss. In a large company such as her's people are asked their opinions about others, so she also knows that she needs to influence positively her workmates, especially the personal assistant of the marketing director. She also notes the positive characteristics that she must exhibit strongly are creativity, commitment to work through longer hours, and speaking up more. At the moment she feels that she lacks a vital spark in all of these areas. On the other hand she knows that she is seen as rather conservative, as not having a good sense of humour nor socialising after work—which tend to mark her down as being a 'bit too straight'. With this self-assessment information, Mary now knows the kind of alterations that she has to make to her image to change her in the eyes of others.

Karen spots the stumbling blocks

Karen has been trying for promotion for years, but she fails each time. The main reason, she thinks, is because her boss considers her a bit 'lightweight'. Because she is always laughing and joking with others, she believes that he considers her not serious enough for a more senior position, even though she does her job well and conscientiously. Having identified this as a possible stumbling block, Karen sets about making herself more serious. In part she does this by 'pressing the buttons' that she knows will influence her boss. First, she knows that he is interested in charitable work so she starts finding out about one of his favourite organisations and drops an occasional mention of the work they are doing into the conversation; when the charity is organising a national day or event she makes sure that she is aware of it and wearing the right badge or similar. She doesn't make a big thing about this, but simply lets her boss absorb it subconsciously. Next, she tones down her clothes, so that they aren't quite so fashionable but are more classical. Eventually she begins to make progress in the company, and once she gets on a roll then she moves quickly ahead.

6
Marketing Yourself Through Words

The right words in the right place and presented in the right way are another important route to successful self-marketing, because they help ensure that the most **effective messages** about you are put across.

Knowing how to write well is important because it helps you get your point of view over to people clearly and confidently, which in turn helps you influence people. You can use your word skills when you write letters, applications, reports and curriculum vitae—which can have a tremendous bearing on how successful you are at self-marketing.

IMPROVING WRITTEN APPLICATIONS

There are many books on how to apply for jobs, so the process of filling in application forms is only briefly covered here.

Standard application forms are not the best way to market yourself because you are being forced to use a format that someone else has decided on, which might not be the best format for you. However, filled in they must be and the following pointers should help you do that better.

- Read carefully all the questions that the application asks. Do so twice so that you don't make mistakes. The applicant who answers a question with totally the wrong information will be considered an idiot for doing so, slapdash in their approach to detail, or not serious about getting the job.

- Before starting to fill in the application, think how you can best select from your background and history to answer the questions on the form. Ask yourself what it is the employer is looking for: it helps to find out as much as you can about their industry and business.

- Write out what you are going to put on the application before you begin filling it in. Don't start filling it in as soon as you receive it.

- Answer all of the questions that are relevant to you. If you can't answer a question say why. Don't leave anyone thinking that you haven't bothered to fill the form in properly or are being evasive. If the question is not relevant to you then fill in the space with 'Not applicable' or 'N/A'.

- Though you should fill in the application in the way that it asks you to, you might like to include a CV which presents you in a better light.

- If there is space left for you to write about yourself then you should always take full advantage by hammering home some of the most relevant points and skills that you have to offer.

- Put a sheet of paper over the parts of the application that you are not writing on so that you don't smudge ink on it.

- Keep the application clean and flat before you fill it in. And even if the application has been folded, send it back flat in a suitably sized envelope.

A high risk strategy

While it is perfectly acceptable to fill in an application form in such a way that you are presented in the best possible manner (that is what self-marketing is all about), you are on a sticky wicket if you actually lie.

If you think you simply aren't qualified enough for a job, or that you haven't quite impressed enough at an interview, then it can be very tempting to bend the truth by claiming that you have done something you have not, for instance. Some cynical people will do this as a matter of course, justifying their actions 'because everyone else is doing it', so they have to lie just to keep pace with everyone else. And though this could be considered an unacceptable attitude indeed, in the short term it can be an effective strategy as long as you aren't found out.

However, if you claim to have some skill which you obviously do not have, then all but the slowest witted around you will soon know it. On the other hand, if you do your job or work well, then you may never be asked about the time you supposedly spent working for a major advertising company, or setting up your own business. And even if you are caught out, if you have done a good job for your employer they may overlook the matter, but you should be warned that if you do lie and are found out, you are probably more likely to be out of a job and without a reference.

IMPROVING YOUR CV

Your curriculum vitae, or CV, is really just your life and career history to date though there are several ways of presenting it, but you need to make sure that your CV shows you in the best light.

Most write their CV in chronological order, starting with their most recent employment, then running backwards to the employment with which they first began working life. An example of a chronological CV is shown in Figure 3.

Writing your CV

Figure 3 shows a relatively simple CV, but there are a number of points worth bringing out.

- A CV should be appropriate to the job you are applying for. You should therefore tailor your CV to the specifications of the job, changing the emphasis where required, omitting some things and including others.

- Don't put Curriculum Vitae at the top of the page. Instead, just put your name, underlined and in capitals at the top of the page. This has more impact.

- At the top of the CV include a mini-profile of yourself and below that a list of your skills (no more than four or five) which you think will be most appropriate for the job.

- Don't include salary details on the CV, as these may change

JOHN SMITH
1 ANYTOWN ROAD, ANYTOWN, ANYTOWNSHIRE AN17 4BB
TEL: 0112 123 456

PROFILE
Experienced advertising copywriter, capable of undertaking wide ranging and varied promotional work including press, radio and television.

KEY SKILLS
—High level copywriting and writing skills
—Good spoken communications
—Ability to master unfamiliar material quickly
—In depth knowledge of wordprocessing packages including Word for
  Windows, WordPerfect and others

EMPLOYMENT
Abracadabra Agency, London   July 1986—Present
Senior copywriter working on a wide range of accounts including
washing machines, cars, hotel chains and microchips.
—Liaised with clients on regular basis.
—Worked on Wonderwash campaign which raised sales of the washing
  powder by 57% in just three weeks!
—Part of presentation team that won Slobberchops Pet Food account.

Quasimodo Agency, London   August 1984—June 1986
'Middleweight' copywriter working on accounts that include hosepipes,
baby food, electronic checkouts, computers and carpets.
—Part of the 'Apples Make Your Hair Grow' creative team which
  increased apple purchases among bald men by 700%.

Freelance writer & editor   February 1981—July 1984
Contributed to a wide range of magazines and newspapers, particularly
writing on subjects such as the environment, computers, financial
matters and watersports. During this three year period had 217 articles
published in 64 publications. Other work includes writing corporate
video scripts.

EDUCATION
1977—80   BA Jt Hons Economics/Economic History University of
            Leicester
1970—77   9 'O' Levels 3 'A' Levels
            Anytown Grammar School, Anytown

PERSONAL
Date of Birth: 10 January 1960   Full driving licence
Marital Status: Single   Good keyboard skills

Fig. 3. A sample CV.

frequently; in any case you don't want to become involved in salary negotiations at this early stage. At the top of the CV include a short profile about yourself. This should be positive and outline in a sentence or two what you do.

- Put the dates you have worked for companies over to the right, this de-emphasises them, something that is important if you think your age may go against you in getting the job, or if you have stayed with some employers for a long time. Similarly, don't draw attention to them by underlining them.

- Don't simply state that you have worked for a company but give some background details about what you did there. Try to include facts and figures which show how you helped the company.

- Keep your CV within two pages, typed and with large margins on good quality white A4 paper.

Professional or DIY CVs?

You can put together your CV yourself or use one of the CV services that advertise themselves either locally or nationally. Some of these are very good, but many are offered by people who are running no more than a glorified typing service and who do not have the skills to help you present your CV in the best way. If you do choose a professional service then make sure that whatever CV they produce:

—is well and simply laid out
—is spelt correctly
—has been laser printed
—includes everything you want
—is not full of double underlines, different typefaces and fancy embellishments.
—is kept on computer file. Then when changes need to be made you won't have to pay someone to rekey all of the text again.

You do not need to pay extra for magnificent binders as they rarely impress any personnel officer or potential employer.

Creating a different CV

Often it can pay to be different when sending out a CV and

application. Think of how a personnel officer must feel spending day in day out looking at virtually identical job applications. How do you think they would react if they came across one that really stood out from the crowd? Especially if you are in a highly competitive line of work, being different can pay dividends, as long as it is within reason and you are not being different for the sake of it. One way to prevent this is to link the style and format of your CV in some way with the industry or business so that it is relevant. See the case history on page 90.

Your referees and references

Referees are very often asked for on applications. And the more credibility the referee has, the more impact your application will have. Consequently **professional people** are very often the best to approach (doctors and lawyers), people at the higher end of the business world (managing directors, financial directors etc) or people who are recognised for their work in the industry you are looking to get into.

Even if referees aren't asked for, don't be frightened to seek and use the support of others in your self-marketing to help you develop your career. If someone says that you have done a good job on something, or a particularly good piece of work, then ask them if they will put this in writing for you. This acts as a testimonial which you can take with you between jobs or to new clients or even include when you send in a CV or application form. Whether the person will do this will very much depend on your relationship with them.

Checklist

Does your application **sell** you in the best way?   Yes/No

Have you answered all the questions on the application form?   Yes/No

Have you brought in all the information that you need to convince the reader that you are the person they are looking for?   Yes/No

Is your CV less than 2 pages long?   Yes/No

Does your CV look attractive?   Yes/No

Does it have wide margins so that it doesn't
look cramped?   Yes/No

Have you enclosed everything that is asked for?   Yes/No

Have you signed everything that you are meant
to sign?   Yes/No

Have you checked grammar and spelling?   Yes/No

WRITING LETTERS THAT SELL YOU

Each CV you send out should be accompanied by a **covering letter**. This draws to the attention of the interviewer any particularly relevant or interesting points about you and your career to date. So you need to see the CV and covering letter as a package.

And while the CV is a rather dry and information-rich document, the covering letter is your chance to do a more personal sales job on yourself. Many of the pointers below apply whatever type of document you are writing.

- Decide who you are writing for. Ask yourself who will read this and what will be the things that 'turn them on'? Try to guess what their attitude will be to what you are writing. Will they be sceptical, enthusiastic, or violently disagree?

- Make a list of all the points that you could make in this piece of writing. If you can, cut the list down to a maximum of five points that you want to get across.

- Try to work out why the reader ought to be interested in each of these points. Ask yourself how each point will benefit them? What will be in it for them?

- A covering letter should point out your suitability for a particular job by highlighting aspects of yourself that are especially beneficial to the employer. This is a straightforward matter of stressing the benefits of a situation rather than just the features.

- If there is no single point for the reader to become really enthusiastic about then try and down-play the negative points by recognising that there is a potential problem, but then pointing out a positive side to it. Consequently you should anticipate any awkward questions that might spring to the interviewer's mind. Remember, the purpose of your application is to get yourself an interview, not the job. You want to remove any seeds of doubt.

- Try to adopt a natural style of writing and avoid 'business speak' at all costs. A natural writing style can quite easily be achieved by using short words and phrases, broken into paragraphs of no more than five or six lines. Use the word 'you' several times at least. This suggests to the reader that you are thinking in terms of their interests.

- Whatever you are writing keep it as brief as possible. Don't think that the more you write the more seriously your document will be taken.

- To create a better impression, not only to the eye, but also to the touch, covering letters should be written on good quality paper, preferably white.

- Give your letter a headline in block capitals and underline it. This is different and saves you space in the body of the letter by telling the reader what the letter is about immediately. For instance, you could print *APPLICATION FOR ASSISTANT MANAGER* at the top of your covering letter and then swoop right into your personal sales pitch.

- Remember to sign off correctly. *Yours sincerely* is right if you address the letter to someone by name. *Yours faithfully* is correct if you are addressing your letter Dear Sir or Madam. To most people this will be immaterial, but at least it shows that you do know the difference and you won't upset the more old-fashioned people to whom it still matters.

- When you sign your letters, do so in blue ink. This makes a pleasant contrast with black type or print, but some research has shown that it also increases response rate. The difference in effectiveness may not be great but every little helps.

- For preference your covering letter should always be typed unless you are specifically asked to send in a handwritten one. The reasons for typing your covering letter are simple and obvious:
  —you can fit more information onto a side of paper if it is typed, which is better than sending out three or four hand-written sheets
  —a typed letter looks more businesslike and professional
  —it shows that you have made the effort and taken the time to type it out
  —it looks more attractive generally than a handwritten letter
  —and it is always clearer to read, something that is especially important if you have bad handwriting.
  However, if a job advertisement asks you for a handwritten covering letter, then you would be foolish to go against the request. If your handwriting is bad all you can do is practise, practise, and keep on writing the letter until you have it as perfect as possible. With handwritten letters it is likely that you will use more than one sheet of paper, so to avoid your chances of making a mistake and having to throw away what you have already written, only write on *one* side of the paper.

WRITING SPECULATIVE LETTERS

So far we have looked at writing letters in reply to specific job advertisements. This is all very well and something that you should do, but by the time you see a job ad, so have many others and you are immediately in competition with them. To get in ahead of the bunch, it can often be worthwhile to write a speculative letter, asking a company whether they have any jobs going.

The advantage of this is that because you aren't applying for a specific job the company may have several for which you would be suitable and you might also save them the effort of advertising and interviewing. After all, what's the point of doing so if they're already looking at someone who has all of the qualifications they need?

The downside of writing speculative letters is that they must hit the right desk at the right time and it is difficult for you to know when that will be. Consequently you probably won't get a very high response rate to a speculative letter, though you can increase your chances of success by using the following plan.

- Speculative letters are virtually identical to covering letters for advertised jobs, only they have to sell the breadth of your skills as you don't know specifically what a company may be looking for.

- If you can, show that you know something about the company by mentioning the products that they make or new business that they have won.

- Really sell your personal good points by stressing the benefits that an employer will derive from them.

- Make your speculative letter visually eye-catching and different.

- Only make your letter funny if you can do so naturally. Not everyone's sense of humour is the same and if yours clashes with theirs you won't be doing yourself any favours.

- Have passport photographs taken of yourself and include one with your speculative letter. Many companies ask for them even with standard applications so it is better to have them to hand so that there is no delay. If you want to spend a little more money then it is worth having photographs professionally taken. However, when you have photographs taken make sure that they show you in your best light: businesslike, professional and smart—not playing the clown or looking as though you have just been dragged out of a morgue. Keep going until you get a shot that is right. Once you have a photograph you can even include it on your applications or speculative letters, photocopying (colour photocopying is particularly effective) the image onto your stationery.

- Try using the direct mail copywriting technique of including a PS at the end of your letter. Research has shown that a PS is one of the most frequently read parts of any letter and it can be a great way not only of catching the eye, but driving home an important point. The PS can be either handwritten or typed. A typed PS is perhaps a little contrived, and so a handwritten one is probably better. It should be written using the same pen that you have used on your signature.

- What to put in the PS? Well, try and avoid putting in anything that should have been a main point in the body of the letter. If you do that, especially with wordprocessed documents, the recipient might think that you just couldn't be bothered to make the change to the letter so as to include the extra information. So ideally the PS should develop a point that you have already made.

The two examples of speculative letters (Figures 4 and 5) show how you can go to town on them if you want. The first one demonstrates an eye catching beginning while the second shows an unusual way of finishing.

To follow up or not?

For the most part it isn't worth following up an application with a phone call. Rarely will a follow up call influence anyone. If your application was good enough to get you an interview you would have heard. However, the exception is with a speculative letter. After all, you weren't applying for any particular job advertised at that moment so it can be worthwhile bringing a little extra selling muscle into the operation. If you do follow up, don't wait too long, three or four days at most, after you think the letter should have landed on someone's desk. If you wait any longer you will lose impact and people will have forgotten about your letter and be busy with other matters.

TRY A SERIES MAILING

Persistence is a fine virtue and you can use it to good effect with a series (perhaps four or five) of speculative letters that effectively build on one another. Pointers to bear in mind are:

THEY'RE LIKE BUSES, AREN'T THEY?

You know how it is. Not a job, project or client around when you need one and then . . . BANG . . . all of a sudden along come several at once. The problem is you want to catch them all *and* maintain your usual quality of service for existing clients. Not the easiest thing in the world to do.

Perhaps that's happening to you right now. Perhaps new clients are knocking at your door or maybe old ones are starting to rattle their bones and demand attention just when your time is limited.

If so, it would be worth giving me a New Year call.

You see, I'm an experienced public relations consultant, highly adaptable and professional, just the sort of person to help you climb on several doubledeckers at once.

(The letter goes on to list points that are of particular interest to the company.)

Fig. 4. The start of a speculative letter.

(Personal sales points are listed here)

When I told my grandmother I was writing this letter, ever the pessimist she said I didn't stand a b***dy chance (I've had to tone down the language, after half a bottle of gin and the high speed blow-out on her walking frame she wasn't in the best of moods). After all, I was probably too old/young, experienced/inexperienced and almost certainly had an incompatible birth sign. (I'm Capricorn, by the way.) What chance did I stand?

Well, all the same I'm writing to you. So why not prove my cantankerous granny wrong, just like old granddad loved to do.

Give me a call. I'll hold my breath until you do.

Yours faithfully

Fig. 5. Another unusual speculative letter.

- The letter should be addressed to the same person each time. The effect of a series mailing comes from its sheer persistence in building up a big picture of you. If each letter goes to someone different you will lose the impact, therefore it's important that you find the right person to mail to before sending off the first letter.

- Write the letters all together so that you see them as one big letter. If you write one letter and then wait to write the next you will find it harder.

- Each letter can have an entirely different style from the previous one. There is one problem. Though you will have a terrific effect if all or most of the letters are kept by the recipient, you will lose impact if they have been thrown away. It is better to keep the layout of every letter the same (you really should have a letterhead or logo); by doing this the recipient immediately recognises that the letter is from you without having to read it.

- You can send out the same letter each time, but this will not be so effective and it will just look as though you can't be bothered to come up with a different one. Try and develop one idea in each letter, with other points developing and supporting it.

MAKING LETTERS LOOK BETTER

Use the best quality writing paper that you can afford. This shows that you are taking your self-marketing seriously and will subconsciously be noticed by the person reading your letter. You will never go wrong with white paper, though a pastel colour—for instance a light cream—will do. But don't use anything stronger than this as it will be difficult to read because you won't have the contrast between the type and paper. It may also lead the recipient to think that you are a bit off the wall. And don't be tempted to pick a paper that has an unusual finish to it, as this can make it difficult for a computer printer or typewriter to turn out clear and crisp characters. Certain finishes can also be difficult to read.

Use the best printer or typewriter available. The sharper and

```
XX XXXXX XXXXXXXX
XXXXXXXXXXX
XXXXXXXXXXX
XXXXXX XXX XXX

XX XXXX XXXXXXXX

XXXXXXXXXXXXXXXXXXXXXXXXXXXXXXX
XXXXXXXXXXXXXXXXXXXXXXXXXXXXXX
XXXXXXXXXXXXXXXXXXXXXXXXXXXXXX
XXXXXXXXXXXXXXXXXXXXXX

XXXXXXXXXXXXXXXXXXXXXXXXXXXXX
XXXXXXXXXXXXXXXXXXXXXXXXXXXXX
XXXXXXXXXXXXXXXXXXXXXXXXX

XXXXXXX XXXXXXX
```

Fig. 6. A well laid-out letter.

```
XX XXXXXX XXXXXXXX
XXXXXXXXXXX
XXXXXXXXXXX
XXXXXXX XXX XXX

XXXXXXXXXXXXXXXXXXXXXXXXXXXXXXXXXX
XXXXXXXXXXXXXXXXXXXXXXXXXXXXXXXXX
XXXXXXXXXXXXXXXXXXXXXXXXXXXXXXXXX
XXXXXXXXXXXXXXXXXXXXXXXXXXXXXXXXX
XXXXXXXXXXXXXXXXXXXXXX

XXXXXXXXXXXXXXXXXXXXXXXXXXXXXXXXXX
XXXXXXXXXXXXXXXXXXXXXXXXXXXXXXXXX
XXXXXXXXXXXXXXXXXXXXXXXXXXXXXXXXXXX
XXXXXXXXXXXXXXXXXXXXXXXXXXXXXXXXX
XXXXXXXXXXXXXXXXXXXXXXXXXXXXXXXXX
XXXXXXXXXXXXXXXXXXXXXXXXXXXXXXXXXX
XXXXXXXXXXXXXXXXXXXXXXXXXXXX

XXXXXXX XXXXXX
```

Fig. 7. A visually unattractive letter.

more like properly printed material you can make your letter look, the more of an impact it will have. If you are using a typewriter then make sure that the ribbon is black and that it is new. You may think that using an old ribbon is economical but it won't make your letter look very good.

Consider indenting the first line of every paragraph. This is easy enough to do if you are using a wordprocessor and can improve the look of a document. You need only indent by five characters or so.

> If you are making a particularly important point then try indenting all of the paragraph that contains it. Just like this one. It makes the point stand out and creates a more interesting visual impression on the page.

While wordprocessors now make it easy to justify text—that is they space words so that the end of every line finishes up against the right hand margin—try to avoid this. This paragraph is justified like this.

> For most documents left justified text, where not every line ends at the right hand margin giving the text a characteristic ragged appearance on the right, is more pleasing to the eye and looks more natural. This paragraph is justified this way.

Use large margins at the top, bottom and sides of the page. This makes any document look better because the eye likes to see plenty of 'white space'. The difference in look between two letters, one with large margins and the other with narrow, can be clearly seen in Figures 6 and 7.

Checklist

Is your letter written from the viewpoint of the person you are sending it to?   Yes/No

Have you stressed benefits about yourself that help the recipient solve their problems?   Yes/No

Is the opening of the letter strong and interesting?   Yes/No

Does it quickly outline the reason you are writing?   Yes/No

Does it contain all the essential information needed to
persuade the other person of your case?   Yes/No

Is the letter written logically with the arguments
well laid out?   Yes/No

Have you included proof in the form of testimonials,
mentions of names, experience and background that
show you will be effective?   Yes/No

Could the letter be shortened and still do its job?   Yes/No

WHEN TO SEND APPLICATIONS AND LETTERS

Ideally you want your application to stand out from the others and
one way of doing this is to ensure that your application doesn't
arrive on someone's desk as one of 30 or 40. If that happens, unless
your application is outstanding, it will be treated as just one of the
crowd.

Responses to any advertised job arrive slowly at first, then
numbers will pick up, reach a peak and trail off again. This is
known as the Bell Curve effect and you can exploit it when you
send in your application. To see why this effect arises, you only
have to think about what happens when people see an ad in the
paper. Unless they are super organised and have the time it will
take between two and four days for them to get their act together
to prepare their application. This means that if the ad appears on
a Monday then the bulk of the applications will come in on
Thursday, Friday, Monday (which will include Saturday's post)
and Tuesday (this will be when most of the applications completed
over the weekend will come in). So, to be different your application
will have to arrive either on Tuesday or Wednesday or after the
following Tuesday. Both options have disadvantages.

If you aim to be early then you may make mistakes in your efforts
to get off a speedy reply. Your application could be swamped by
the deluge of responses after it. If your application is 'late' then it
has a greater chance of being noticed because by this time the
company should have a good idea of the quality of the applicants:

this gives you a chance to stand out. On the other hand, an uncharitable personnel officer might consider you were too disorganised to send in an application any earlier.

If a 'reply by' date is given, then try to ensure that your letter will arrive about three quarters of the way through the time allowed. By this time the bulk of the applications will be in, but you won't be seen as a 'last minute' applicant.

If an ad gives only a phone number then you should phone it as soon as possible. The company is obviously in a rush to fill a vacancy and may have allocated the staff on this one day only to handle incoming calls from job seekers. What is more, if the ad is particularly successful, with 100 people or more calling in the morning, then the company may decide that they are bound to be able to appoint someone from those who have already phoned and simply say that the vacancy is filled.

When you get through to the company either they will ask for your name and address and send you an application form or information pack, or they will use your phone call as an exercise to assess your suitability. To make sure that you aren't caught out, jot down a few notes on your relevant skills and qualifications before picking up the phone.

Mailing your application or letter

Whenever you have the option, always send your application unfolded in a large envelope (320mm x 230mm) which will take a sheet of standard A4 paper. There are several reasons for doing this.

- First, a larger envelope has more impact when it lands on someone's desk, especially if everyone else is sending in their applications folded up in small envelopes.

- Second, flat papers create a better impression when they are on someone's desk. This is subconsciously taken in by the person looking at your application.

- Third, it tends to show that you are treating your application seriously by not damaging it with folds.

If you suspect that your envelope will hit the desk of the person you are sending it to without first being opened, then you should use a good quality envelope. A white or cream coloured envelope looks better than a standard brown one. If you want to increase your chances of your letter reaching a decision maker than you can always write 'Private and Confidential' on the front of the envelope. This should ensure that it gets by all but the most trusted of secretaries and mailroom staff. This can backfire, however, if the person you are sending it to thinks that you are a 'trickster'.

However, good envelopes can be expensive and they can be wasted if all mail is opened by a secretary who immediately throws away the envelopes. So, if it is a toss-up between spending money on envelopes or on writing paper, go for the writing paper.

IMPROVING YOUR WORD POWER

Good writing generally isn't about using big or clever words. Indeed, this is generally counter-productive because many people won't know what you are talking about and the message you are trying to put across will be obscured. However, you need to improve your word power so that you know when to use the correct word and so that you don't confuse one word with another of different meaning. You can improve your word power by broadening the range of books that you read and always looking up in the dictionary any words that you don't understand. Then, when you have done this write these new words and their meaning down in a notebook, which you can regularly review. Doing this will quickly increase your vocabulary.

CASE HISTORIES

Jane uses an imaginative approach

Jane has chosen a field of work where there is always a lot of competition for job vacancies with perhaps literally hundreds hitting the personnel officer's desk whenever they advertise a job. And though her qualifications and experience are pretty good, Jane knows that when you are dealing with such numbers getting the job becomes something of a lottery, that may depend on the personal preferences of the personnel officer, or how they are feeling at that moment. So, to make her application stand out, she gets an artistic friend to create a CV for her that shows her career history in the form of a cartoon story (she could equally well have done it in the form of a newsletter, a brochure, or a storyboard). The result is dramatic and catches the eye of nearly every company it goes to. Of course, Jane knows that she will miss out on some jobs because it will be thought of as too gimmicky, but she does find that overall the number of interviews she is called for increases.

Jerry thinks laterally

Wanting to make himself different for a marketing job, Jerry writes his covering letter as though it were a press release for a product. This approach is not only different from most other applications, but it shows that Jerry knows the basics of writing a press release, which could be useful. If Jerry had been going for a job in a PR agency, where press releases are written every day, this might be seen as a rather hackneyed and overdone approach.

How to Write a CV That Works

Paul McGee

What makes a CV stand out from the crowd? How can you present yourself in the most successful way? This practical book shows you how to develop different versions of your CV for every situation. Reveal your hidden skills, identify your achievements and learn how to communicate these successfully. Different styles and uses for a CV are examined, as you discover the true importance of your most powerful marketing tool. Paul McGee is a freelance Trainer and Consultant for one of Britain's largest outplacement organisations. He conducts Marketing Workshops for people from all walks of life.

£7.99. 128 pp illus. 1 85703 171 7.

Please add postage & packing (UK £1 per copy,
Europe £2 per copy, World £3 per copy airmail).

How To Books Ltd, Plymbridge House, Estover Road, Plymouth PL6 7PZ,
United Kingdom. Tel: (01752) 695745. Fax: (01752) 695699. Telex: 45635.

Credit card orders may be faxed or phoned.

7
How to Market Yourself Face to Face

You will need to be convincing in front of interviewers, your boss and work colleagues if you want to market yourself effectively. And what you say and how you say it can play a decisive part in doing that. Therefore it is crucially important that you know and understand the techniques that will impress others.

MINDING YOUR (BODY) LANGUAGE

Everyone communicates in three basic ways:

- by the words we use

- by how we say those words

- and by what our bodies say.

You may find it surprising, but on many occasions the way our body talks, our body language, says far more than our words or the way that we say them. And yet it is an area to which many people pay little attention or heed.

Avoiding bad body language

You may believe that you are the most important thing in the world since the invention of sliced bread but if your body is telling everyone the complete opposite—that you are uncomfortable, lack confidence and are a general loser—they will subconsciously pick up on your body message. They may not know why they are rejecting your proposal, your application or your scheme, but reject it they will.

Likewise you are sure to have been near someone who is very nervous. You will probably have noticed that they are all twisted up, with legs crossed and arms folded, and their face screwed up into a ball of tension. Immediately you knew that that person was nervous, even if they denied it in a voice that was controlled and confident.

Therefore, if you want to make a good impression you need to make sure that you are in control of your body especially if it is likely to contradict what you are saying.

How to Market Yourself is not a treatise on body language, so these are only some of the basic body language signals that you should avoid if you want to create a good impression.

Suppress mannerisms

Don't fidget or display nervousness by using excessive or irritating mannerisms. These might include twiddling your thumbs, tugging at your hair or continually sweeping it back, picking at your nails or at imaginary bits of fluff on your trousers. Instead, sit back in your chair making certain that you aren't slouching in it. Don't let your feet slide out in front of you. Clasp your hands in front of you and keep them gently lying in your lap. If you feel you must do something with your hands you can always take notes of what other people are saying. However, you should only really do this if it is appropriate to do so. If you do take notes then be careful not to doodle: if you are bored or distracted this is one sure-fire way of telling people so.

Leave your face alone

Don't put your hands up to your face. Very often most people don't even realise that they are tapping at the side of their nose, gently fondling their ear lobes, or rubbing at their eyes, but research into each of these gestures has shown that we tend to think that each of these indicates that a person is lying. That may not be the case at all, but if the other person thinks so, then you have a problem.

Don't use props

Don't take off your spectacles and start cleaning them in the middle of the meeting and likewise don't light up a pipe or a cigarette, even if the person you are with smokes like a chimney. Often such activities come across as stalling tactics designed to gain you time, probably because you don't know what you are talking about, or because you are a bundle of nerves.

Don't fold your arms

Don't fold your arms across your chest or stomach. This makes you look defensive, protecting your position against what the other person is trying to tell you. This is the attitude of the person who will not be moved, or has something to hide.

Watch your hands

Don't use both your hands to hold a bag or cup in front of you. Again this is a defensive position and creates the impression that you are lacking in confidence and generally feeling unsure of yourself. If you are offered a cup of tea or coffee put it down on the floor or on a nearby table when you've finished with it. When you are holding the cup and saucer, keep it on your lap, not in front of your chest or stomach.

These are just a few of the basic elements to look out for in your own body language when marketing yourself. And always remember that these gestures work two ways, so look out for them in other people. In particular keep a watch on their facial expressions, hand movements and body position and take confidence from the fact that they may be more nervous than you.

One further point. Body language can be a great help in indicating the attitudes and beliefs of others, but it shouldn't be relied on exclusively. Scratching the side of the nose may mean that someone is lying; it may also mean that they have an itch there!

Using good body language

Use your hands positively

In meetings and interviews don't be frightened to use hands and arms to make gestures if you would do this normally to emphasise a point, though don't go overboard and become a human windmill.

Make your eyes work for you

If you find that when in conversation your eyes temporarily drift away from the other person, don't worry. This is perfectly normal and something that you can use to your advantage, if after your eyes have drifted away, you bring them back to focus on the other person, pause and then make your point. This makes you seem more serious and gives extra weight and impact to your words.

Be enthusiastic
When someone makes a point to you, smile and nod. This suggests that you understand their point of view and way of thinking. Also smile as you speak and be as enthusiastic as you can. If you aren't enthusiastic about what you're telling someone, why expect *them* to be?

Use your voice effectively
When it comes to talking about figures or other important items, you need a more serious approach, which you can achieve by lowering your voice. When she wanted to increase her effectiveness as a politician and make herself more of a 'statesman', Margaret Thatcher dramatically lowered her voice.

GETTING ON BETTER WITH PEOPLE

Think before you speak. If you just open your mouth and let words spew out, neither you nor the people who are listening to you will really know what you mean. Once said, wrong words can't be unsaid. Sometimes this doesn't matter, but at other times it matters a great deal.

Listen to what others are saying and never be tempted to shout them down. Respect their points of view. Nobody likes being beaten around the head by someone else's point of view. In any case, if you don't listen carefully to what others are saying then you may well find yourself giving them incorrect information, arguing on the wrong point and generally working yourself into a lather of disagreement when they may actually be agreeing with you. Again, you can show that you are listening to what others are saying by nodding your head and making little sounds of agreement at appropriate points. You should also look at the speaker while you do this or they will still think that you *aren't* listening to them.

Look for similarities between you and others. Develop a rapport by mentioning games that you both like, talking about their children, their families, mutual interests and hobbies.

If you disagree on some things, then stress any positive elements about the situation. Focusing on these will diminish the importance of the negative side of things and change the whole tone of a meeting, moving it away from a feeling of pessimism to a more optimistic stance. Often this will reveal that things may not be quite as bad as everyone thought.

If there are things everybody disagrees about and you all know this, state this openly at the beginning, so the problem is out in the open. Everyone will work more easily then.

If you don't understand something, say so. Don't muddle through in ignorance. Taking things for granted has caused many a problem in its time.

Action point

Read different books on body language and begin studying the people that you see about you. What can you tell from their body language? But remember not to rely exclusively on body language signals—you can be misled. Use it in conjunction with your own common sense.

Make a conscious effort not to adopt negative body postures yourself that send out the wrong signals about you.

Put these principles of body language into practice by applying for a few jobs that you *don't* want. Then, if you get the interviews you will have some valuable experience of creating the right impression with no risk of failing because you don't want the job anyway.

IMPROVING YOUR VOICE

Why change your voice?

The voice is just another aspect of our image and personality, and this may or may not be to your advantage. These are some of the reasons that you might want to change your voice:

- it sounds juvenile so people don't take you seriously

- it is so quiet that people can't hear you and constantly ask you to repeat yourself or to speak up

- you don't speak clearly enough so others have to ask you to repeat yourself

- it doesn't have any confidence and so makes you sound weak and ineffective

- it is strongly regional so people aren't sure what it is you are saying

- it is very flat so comes across as being boring

- you use too many ums and ers (most of us do), which makes listening to you uncomfortable, difficult and tedious.

What do others think of your voice (Ask them to be as specific as possible)?

. . . .

. . . .

. . . .

How to improve your voice

You may have a certain voice because of the structure of your vocal cords and the influences of others' accents where you grew up but you still can do something about your voice. Making the appropriate changes can have a significant impact on your success.

But this isn't all about changing your voice to sound posh. Indeed, talking as though you have a plum in your mouth can be counterproductive because the more 'extreme' your voice the less others will take you seriously and the more difficult they will find it to relate to you.

So, a 'good' voice should be easy to listen to, be interesting, have a certain power and a persuasive quality and instil confidence in others. With these characteristics in your voice you will be more effective in interviews, and during any speeches and sales presentations that you might have to make.

Voice changing tactics

Most people's voices could do with a little work so think about putting into practice the following techniques:

- Choose someone with a good voice and listen carefully to them. This could be someone you know, but it is easier to choose a person you hear regularly on television or radio. Be careful to select someone whose voice you feel comfortable with. You don't want to end up with a voice that sounds obviously false or forced. But don't necessarily try and copy what they say and the way that they say it, rather pay attention to the rhythm, the tone and depth of the voice. Repeat phrases and sentences to get the balance, intonation and emphasis right.

- Practise speaking carefully, precisely and clearly from a book in front of a mirror. Most people are self-conscious about this so wait until no one's around before doing this as it's important that you open your mouth properly and don't mumble. Try and get an up and down rhythm to your voice as this makes it more interesting. Think of how the good speaker you are copying talks.

- If you don't already have one, beg, steal or borrow a tape recorder and record yourself reading a page or two from this book. When you have finished play the tape back. Yes, that really is how you speak. Now what are the good points and bad points about your voice? What do you think? What do others think? Is it lazy, does it sound slurred, nervous, hesitant, too loud or too soft? Now read the same pages again but bear these points in mind: make a real effort to open your mouth a little wider than you do normally. Your throat will feel a little more open too. Smile. Then try and alter the tone of your voice so that it goes up and down. Listen to the tape again. Now doesn't that sound better? Keep practising. When you have recorded your voice, keep the tapes, as they will serve as indication of the progress that you have made.

- Read books on voice control and pay particular attention to what they have to say about breathing. If you are more serious about developing your voice then consider taking lessons from a voice coach.

- When you feel more confident about your voice then take every opportunity to speak in front of others, just small groups at first, but then larger groups as you feel more comfortable.

- If your voice tends to rise even higher when you speak to others and your words become more rapid then make a conscious effort to slow down your breathing and to take deeper breaths. Relax your shoulders as you do so. Also make a deliberate effort to slow down your speech. If you are still rushing your words, practise taking a few deep breaths (not too obviously) between sentences.

SPEAKING IN PUBLIC

Being able to speak or present information confidently in front of others can be a turning point in one's career. If you carry it off you will appear professional, in command of your work, and persuasive. If you don't then you will be seen to be incompetent, unprofessional and, well, just not up to it.

To increase your chances of being in the first category rather than the second you should remember these few basic rules:

- Try not to speak too fast. Your voice may now sound persuasive and confidence inspiring, but if you deliver what you have to say in a machine gun fashion, it makes it very difficult for listeners to follow and understand what you are saying. And if they don't understand, they will lose interest very quickly in you. Fast speakers also face the possibility that they won't be taken seriously. Indeed, some comedians use a rapid fire delivery to enhance their comic technique.

- Pause frequently as you deliver the speech. The pauses can be at natural points in a sentence, at the end of a sentence, or after an interruption, for instance if someone asks a question.

- Try to 'say' your words rather than just speaking them. The more you can do this the more natural will your words sound and the more impact they will have on the audience.

- Attempt to 'project' your voice to the very back of the room, if you are talking to quite a number of people. If you are facing everybody around a table this won't be necessary, unless the table is very large. Projecting your voice does require practice and is a combination of breath control and having the confidence to raise your voice so you will be heard.

- Lower the pitch of your voice so that it is not too high. If it is then people will find you difficult to listen to and your voice won't carry so far. A high pitched voice is a particular problem for women.

- Give your voice as much variety as you can by changing the emphasis of different parts of a sentence, trying to match the content of your words to the tone of your voice. Flat and monotonous voices soon lose the interest of those listening to them. In the worst cases monotonous voices will literally send the audience to sleep.

Action point

Practise reading out loud any piece of written material. It doesn't matter where it has come from: it could be a magazine article, Charles Dickens or a cornflake packet.

Tell a friend that you are looking to improve your voice and ask them to listen while you read. Get their comments on the way that you sound and on how they feel you could improve your voice. Do they think that you speak too slowly, quickly, hesitantly or what? You need someone who is going to take this exercise seriously and whom you can trust to be honest and unbiased. Do the same thing again but extend the listening group to three or four.

Identify a topic or subject you're interested in. This could be a hobby, a football team, or even a person. Now, write a short two or three minute talk on that subject and deliver this to your listening group. Once you have done this a few times with different subjects, try the same thing with a longer talk.

Take any opportunities you can get to talk informally in front of others. This could be at meetings of your football or tennis club, for example. When you have some confidence in doing this then you could look for more formal talking opportunities, such as invitations to talk to the WI about your hobbies. If you are asked, just say 'yes' and don't think about it.

CASE HISTORIES

Thomas finds a hidden talent

Thomas is to be best man at his brother's wedding. But though he is very flattered and honoured to be asked, he is worried about having to make the traditional best man's speech since he has never done any public speaking before. As the day approaches, Thomas is filled with a deepening dread about his speech, even though he has written it carefully and others think it's funny. Indeed, he almost backs out.

When the day comes he finds that he actually likes public speaking. People laugh at his jokes and respond to his words and he gets a real burst of adrenalin and on sitting down he receives a genuine and well deserved round of applause. Thomas is hooked and can't wait for the next opportunity to speak in public. Like so many others, Thomas has found that his fear of public speaking is actually much worse than actually doing it. Indeed, public speaking can be fun . . . if you let it.

Roger should recognise his limitations

While Thomas discovered that he liked speaking in public, Roger, the managing director of a smallish engineering company, has always adored standing up and speaking in front of others. There is only one problem, he isn't very good at it. This doesn't matter too much when he makes a speech at the golf or Rotary Club, but it does at work. Unfortunately for his company Roger always insists on making the presentations and sales pitches to prospective clients and suppliers. The result? They're bored to death in ten minutes and looking for reasons not to give their business to Roger's company, while all the time a frustrated marketing manager, who's good at public speaking, sits silently by. Roger has fallen into the trap of many people, believing that he is good at something when he is not. If you think that public speaking will benefit you, don't assume that you are good at it: find out from others and improve your skills. You may have confidence in your own abilities but you should never give up learning.

8
Other Self-Marketing Methods

Other than in standard ways, such as writing CVs and covering letters and filling in application forms, many people don't look to market themselves at all. But there are many techniques that can be adapted from the world of business to give you, your career and ambitions a boost. This chapter looks at just a few of them.

SELF-MARKETING THROUGH MEETINGS

Meeting people is a great way of marketing yourself. Why? First, it lets you talk to people who can help you directly by offering you jobs and by becoming potential employers or clients. And second, if these people can't help you directly then they may be able to do so indirectly by suggesting others who can.

You may think that 'using people' like this is rather underhand, but it's not, especially if you are prepared to return the favour or kindness in some other way. Those who 'milk the system' by taking and never giving back tend to lose out in the long run because others begin to see them as leeches, and eventually cease to offer any more help or advice.

Where to meet helpful people:

Local business associations and clubs
Most towns and counties have them. Their regular meetings can provide an invaluable means of meeting new contacts and of obtaining information on what interesting opportunities there may be locally.

Conferences and events

These not only help you with obtaining information about potential employers, but they will also tell you a great deal about that particular industry. Additionally, when in conversation with potential employers at a later date you can say you were at an event or show, which demonstrates your interest and gives you a topic to discuss. For the most part you shouldn't be visiting an event with a view to obtaining a job there and then, but if the opportunity arises to talk about your interest in a company or an industry and a job opportunity is mentioned then go for it.

Courses

These are another valuable means of making new contacts while at the same time hopefully learning something new.

Action point

Read the business news in the local newspapers and in magazines and local Chamber of Commerce, TEC or other business organisations' publications. Begin making a list of the business meetings that are going on in the area:

. . . .
. . . .
. . . .
. . . .

Which of these local events, conferences or meetings are you going to go to?

. . . .
. . . .
. . . .

NETWORKING

A more organised approach to using the experience and positions of others is to network. Read the local press and find out who is who in the industry or type of business that you are interested in. Write their names down here:

. . . .

For each name work out a way in which you might be able to meet them at a social or business event. For instance, do you know anyone who knows them already?

Imagine that you have attended a business meeting which they are at. How would you begin a conversation with them?

How could you develop the conversation to your advantage?

What information could you find out about them and their business beforehand with which you could show your knowledge of their world?

Extending your network

Once you have got into the habit of meeting people, 'networking', then you should begin to spread your net, using one person to make contact with another. Remember though, if you are not to be seen as a bloodsucker, be prepared to offer something (not a bribe) in return. And once in position stay in touch with your network regularly. If you have any information that they might find useful (and which won't lead to accusations of telling tales) pass it on. This always gives you a good reason for calling them up and stops them thinking you are using them. If you contact people only when you want something from them, they will soon be less than happy with your calls. And when you do make contact with people in your network, keep the call or visit short. You and they are both busy. You can have longer social sessions when necessary.

Once you have set up one network, you needn't stop there. You can have as many networks of contacts as you like, one for each different aspect of your life.

DEVELOPING A PERSONAL PR PROGRAMME

For many businesses **public relations** can be one of the most cost effective ways of promotion. The same applies to individuals. So far, in every chapter of *How to Market Yourself* a subconscious acknowledgement has been made to personal public relation because that is very much what this book is about, creating an image for yourself that others respond to in a positive light.

One of the main vehicles of standard PR is using the power of the press to raise a company's profile. You can do the same:

- Appear in the local press. Having your picture and a write up about you in the local press does wonders for raising your profile locally. You immediately become somebody (at least for a week) simply because the paper has thought you important enough to write about. It doesn't really matter why you are in the news (unless it is for something illegal or immoral), just that you are. Being good at sports, becoming involved with a local charity, or campaigning about a local issue (as long as it is not too controversial) are all good ways of getting in the local newspaper. And there may be subsequent opportunities to appear on local radio and television, who tend to follow up stories they read in the local press. If you can't be part of the news then you can at least write in a letter to the editor about the local news. It perhaps isn't much, but it's a start.

- Write magazine or newspaper articles. If you know quite a lot about a subject then consider writing an article about it. Your name should appear as the author and to an extent this makes you an immediate expert on the subject and improves your professional credibility and marketing potential.

- Write a book or books. This requires a similar approach to writing an article, but needs a more major commitment in terms of your time and effort. There are plenty of books around on writing, including *How to Write for Publication* in this series.

You should find that *How to Do Your Own PR* in this series will give you a wider and more in-depth idea of how you can use PR to your personal advantage.

How to make yourself an expert

Making yourself an expert on a certain subject or subjects can give your self-marketing efforts a real boost as experts are always in demand to comment on events and situations. This leads to lots of publicity and promotional opportunities. Beginning to make yourself an expert is really just an extension of your general personal public relations programme.

Choose a subject carefully

Decide on the subject you want to be seen as an expert in. If you are fortunate you will already know something about this; however, if you are making a positive career move then you might have to strike off into areas you as yet know nothing about. So do a little crystal ball gazing and try to predict the subject areas that might be important in a couple of years' time. This will give you a little time for your education and give you an advantage over those who didn't look so far ahead. However, always be on the look out for topical opportunities; if a whole new area seems to be becoming popular and worthy of media attention, then think about delving into that. However, there is no point becoming an expert in an area that is already saturated with them. Ideally, look for an area which you can have all to yourself for a time at least.

Do your homework

Having decided upon your specialist area than start your education by first reading general, basic books and then broadening your reading to take in more complex publications. Attend lectures, talks and go to trade shows where appropriate. This won't be easy, and will take effort on your part; however in a few months you should have a good grounding. Then you can start bringing yourself up to date by reading trade journals and publications. These will give you an idea of the 'names' within this subject area and the current topics that are being talked about.

Start networking

Join clubs, organisations and associations connected with your subject and begin meeting and networking with people. When talking to them start developing your own ideas about current issues. Begin making moves to become 'someone' in the organisation.

Go public

When you are more confident in your knowledge then start a personal campaign of writing letters to the trade journals about particular issues. Don't just agree with what someone else has said, but take the debate forward by suggesting new areas to be discussed. In all of this don't be a shrinking violet. Express your views strongly—this will get you noticed more and, if your ideas are good, may well result in you being asked by the magazine to write an article. In any case, there is no reason why you should not approach the publication directly with an article idea. All you need do is write suggesting the idea to the magazine's editor, the angle and direction it would take and your qualifications for writing the piece. When you have an article or a letter published cut it out and keep a scrapbook of your written work.

Recognising success

If you maintain a high profile for long enough, eventually people should start recognising you as a personality or a name in your industry or business. You will know when that happens because journalists will start asking you for your opinions and comments. You know now that you are seen as an expert. Others may know more about a subject that you do, but your self-marketing efforts have ensured that the media will think of you when they need information.

Once you have become recognised in your own industry then you can begin widening the scope of your self-marketing by putting together an information pack on yourself, your background and your qualifications which can be sent out to newspapers and radio and television stations.

ADVERTISING YOURSELF

Self-advertising is more expensive than PR because you actually have to buy space in the press; placing a 'work wanted' ad in the local, regional or even national newspapers or journals can be a winner, though you are more likely to achieve success if you are involved in an unusual area of work or have interesting or sought after skills. If you just have general skills then you will probably be more effective marketing yourself in other ways.

Over several weeks look at work wanted ads in the local and national newspapers and trade journals. Which of the ads catches your eye? Ask other people if they have any personal preferences. They may be able to give you an insight into the thinking of employers, especially if they are employers themselves.

Set yourself a budget for your advertising. Then call the newspaper and find out what different sizes of ad cost. The ad doesn't have to be massive in size, but avoid very small ones as they won't leave you enough space to say anything other than 'Man wants work'.

You can use several different strategies, either placing the same ad in several different publications or the same (or different) ad several weeks running in the same paper. However, you can only run the same ad once or twice. If people see the same ad appearing week after week then it is pretty obvious that either you aren't being successful, or employers have tried you out and find you wanting. You can use the same ad if you are in the market for repeatable freelance work, in which case they may think the ad is proving a success and that is why you keep it running.

Remember always to include a contact telephone number or address where you can be easily reached. You can use a box number, but this might put people off.

To make your ad really striking you could even include a photograph, but this would need to be professionally taken as you'll always lose some of the quality when it is printed on coarse paper. If your ad is eye catching enough then the story about your endeavours to find work may even be picked up on in the editorial columns of that paper, or others.

A self-marketing business card

Business cards are a great way of introducing yourself to someone (the Japanese do this all the time) and for leaving vital information about yourself with others in a professional and easy manner.

If your company doesn't supply you with business cards have one done up for yourself. Check for company rules which prevent you putting the company logo or even your position onto non-standard or unapproved literature.

Your business cards should be standard size, with your name and telephone number included along with a slogan that explains what you do, such as 'Highly creative interior design', 'Cost effective Public Relations', or 'Plumbing Engineer'.

You don't need to have very costly business cards, but cheap and nasty ones do leave a bad impression, so get the best you can afford. If you can, have them professionally designed, perhaps with a logo, rather than just typesetting. For an even more distinctive marketing device you can have postcards printed. These give you more scope for developing a design, more room for copy and are certainly more memorable.

Even if you are unemployed you can still use business cards to market yourself. They should indicate what it is you used to do, or what you hope to do.

CREATING A SELF-MARKETING FILE

At an early stage of your work or business career, you should set up a self-marketing file. This is really no more than a folder into which you drop any notes or ideas you have about marketing yourself, thoughts on how to handle interview questions, layouts and formats for CVs etc, work that you are proud of, press cuttings about yourself and the like. Look through your self-marketing file regularly and make use of the information it holds.

A variation of the self-marketing file is the **portfolio**, also known as 'books', which are really scrapbooks of the work you have done. You don't need a proper portfolio folder (if you do they can be bought from art supply shops), but can make do with a large ring binder, or something similar, which contains materials (examples of your work, photographs etc) in clear plastic envelopes. If you use photocopies of your work then they should be good quality and not dog-eared.

Update your self-marketing files, work portfolio and CV regularly and before you need to. This will save you a lot of time because inevitably you seem to end up applying for jobs or having to pitch for new work when you are at your busiest and have less time than usual. Having to do little to your CV or portfolio to support your approach or application means that you can mail out an application very quickly or attend an interview at short notice.

Action point
Begin to set up your self marketing file immediately. As you gather together more and more information about yourself remember to add it to your file and portfolio.

MARKETING YOURSELF WHEN UNEMPLOYED

Especially if you have been unemployed for some time it is very easy to become lost in all the empty time that seems to stretch out around you. And because there is no real structure to your day you just drift along. If you are to be good at self-marketing yourself you mustn't let this happen, so:

- Go on a marketing blitz immediately. Successful self-marketing is often just a numbers game. The more letters you send out, the more phone calls you make, the more people you meet the greater the likelihood that you will connect with an opportunity that can move you forward. Another benefit of thinking in terms of numbers is that each individual call, letter or person becomes less important in your overall plan. Contrast that with the situation when you send out only a few letters of application. Each one then takes on an undue importance with you temporarily 'paralysed', waiting to hear whether you have been successful, and then falling into a depression when you hear that you have not. So think numbers and link them into targets that you are going to achieve.

- Set yourself a target number of application letters you will send off this week.

- Get yourself on a roll by being extra active. If you can't find enough things to do to keep yourself permanently busy with your self-marketing then do things in batches so that you work solidly for an hour or two rather than spread things out over the day or week. This will get you used to working in

concentrated bursts of activity. You will also be more efficient
and productive in this way.

Action point

Write down the target number of self-marketing letters you
are going to send out in the next week: . . . .

Write down the target number of applications you are going
to send out in the next week: . . . .

Write down the number of self-marketing phone calls you are
going to make in the next week: . . . .

Whether you are unemployed or not ask yourself how you can
market yourself better in the next two/four/six/twelve months? List
20 answers. Do this three days running so that you have 60 answers
by the end. This is not only a good way of giving you many useable
ideas, but it also is highly beneficial in terms of developing your
creativity and imagination.

CASE HISTORY

Jan tries a bold approach

Jan has taken a very dramatic step in her self-marketing campaign.
She is trying to impress a small advertising agency in the Midlands
that she is a good designer with loads of imagination. But no matter
how many speculative letters she sends she always gets the brush
off. This is very annoying for her because she has some inside
gossip that the agency is not very happy with one of its three
designers. So Jan takes the dramatic step of approaching the
company who own the building opposite and asking them if she
can unfurl out of their window a poster she has designed which
extolls her virtues. The poster gets a lot of reaction, not only from
people from the advertising agency but also from people in the
street who stop to look at it. And you've guessed it, Jan lands a
job not with the stubborn advertising agency, but with the
publishing house whose windows she used. Self-marketing can
often take unusual routes.

9
Organising Your Marketing

It's all very well having a marketing plan for yourself, but it is next to useless if you don't put it into operation because you aren't managing yourself or organising your time properly. This chapter is all about the techniques and methods to help you do just that.

CREATING A SELF-MARKETING TIME

The amount of time you need to set aside to market yourself depends on what you want to achieve, your ambitions and your personal circumstances.

If you are currently unemployed then you will presumably have more time available to spend on self-marketing than if you already have a job. But whatever your situation you should set aside a **regular** time either each day or each week when you will make a concerted effort to market yourself.

Ideally this time should be one when you are free from interruption and disturbance so that you can concentrate fully—and because it always takes us some time to warm up and to 'get our act together'.

Try to set aside an hour in your week. This is your self-marketing 'magic hour' and you should make it a habit. Before you start your magic hour, write down the five things that it would make you happy to do in that hour: important things that you have been putting off doing but which you could at least make a start on during the hour.

When to create marketing time
Self-marketing can be a pretty intensive business and so to achieve the most from your efforts this time should be when you are at your best. That is in the morning if you are a 'lark' or in the

Your sleep alertness table

	6-8	8-10	10-12	12-2	2-4	4-6	6-8	8-10
Alert & energetic	I	I	I	I	I	I	I	I
Alert but not at peak	2	2	2	2	2	2	2	2
Awake, not full alert	3	3	3	3	3	3	3	3
Sluggish	4	4	4	4	4	4	4	4

Fig. 8. A sleep/alertness table.

evening, or even at night, if you are an 'owl'. If you aren't sure when you are at your best then use the method described here to find out.

Start filling in the table above. Just ring the number in each line that describes most accurately the way you feel at that time. Do this throughout the day, every two hours. For example, if you feel alert and energetic at eight in the morning, ring the I for that time. But if you feel lethargic at that time then circle the 4.

At the end of a week you should see a pattern emerging. For instance, you might have circled a lot of Is in the mornings which means you are a lover of early mornings, a lark. On the other hand you might have circled a number of Is in the evening, which means you are an owl, so it will be sensible to do a lot of your concentrated work in the evenings.

USING SELF-MARKETING LISTS

Writing out lists is one of the very best ways of making sure that you do the things you have to do. List making is used by many successful people and you can certainly employ it to good use when marketing yourself. Lists work because they give you the physical evidence of your intentions but also cause a pang of guilt when you don't do them. There is the fateful item staring back at you from the page. What is more, it may only be a simple pleasure, but most of us get a real thrill of achievement when we cross another item off our lists.

How to make a list
Making a list of things to do is a pretty straightforward activity, but by following these five steps you should do a better job still.

Step 1
Take 15 or 20 minutes to make a list of all the things that you want to do tomorrow that will help market you. The best time to do this is at the end of a working day or in the evening. The jobs that you might want to put down are: find out the name of a company's personnel officer; visit the library and make a list of 20 local companies; spend 20 minutes practising your speaking skills; write a CV; or fill in an application. This is List 1.

Step 2
Once a week write out a list of all the longer term jobs that you want or have to do. These jobs might include going on a course to learn a new skill, planning a new wardrobe, or improving the presentation of your CV. These are jobs that you probably won't be doing tomorrow but which need to be done in the near future. Some of these you might need to break down into smaller jobs which are easier to manage and so that they can be done in just a few minutes or perhaps an hour. For example, you might want to break putting a display of your work together into chunks such as, gathering all the material together, writing any supporting captions that need doing, or buying a folder. Each of these is a small job in itself, but which when once done takes you nearer to finishing the whole job. This is your List 2.

Step 3
To create a final 'To Do' list you will need to move some of the jobs from List 2 onto List 1. By doing this you ensure that every day you manage to take a step or two nearer to your longer term goals and aims. Be careful about making this final list too long. If you do that, the chances are you won't finish everything on it by the end of the day and you will become demoralised. If items are left on the list at the end of the day, transfer them to the next. However, if you find you are transferring the same items from day

to day then you're probably guilty of putting off these jobs for some reason.

Step 4

When you have made up your final list you can then go down it and work out how important each item is. If it is important mark it A, if it is slightly less important, mark it B, and if it is a bottom of the pile job then mark it C. However, a faster way to prioritise the list is to choose the most important item on the list and then do it. And when you have finished it you just choose the next most important item until you have finished the list.

Step 5

After you have chosen to do an item on the list you should then just do it.

Like anything else, you will become better at making and using

Daily timetable		**Date** _____
Start		*Duration (minutes)*
8.00		
8.10		
8.20		
8.30		
8.40		
8.45		
9.00		
9.15		
9.30		
9.45		
9.50		
10.00		
10.15		

Fig. 9. Framework for a daily self-marketing timetable.

lists the more often you do it. You will also begin to discover your own particular ways of applying these hints.

CREATING A DAILY SELF-MARKETING TIMETABLE

Lists are a great means of helping you organise yourself, but they are best used with a daily **timetable** which helps give a more rigid structure and framework to your day. This can be particularly important if you are unemployed or have generally just got out of the rhythm of doing things.

When you create a timetable you should plan to fill only 60 to 70 per cent of your available time. If you try to fill up your entire day down to the last second you won't leave any room for the unexpected. With 30 to 40 per cent of 'slack' in your day you have some flexibility.

You'll need a sheet of A4 paper and your To Do list to create your timetable. On the paper draw up a grid like the one shown here.

This timetable shows part of the day (the morning), divided into blocks of time. These blocks can be of 10, 15, 20 or 30 minutes. Don't work in longer blocks than this because you probably won't be able to concentrate. Using smaller time blocks also means you have more flexibility. If you want you can even use different lengths of time blocks for different parts of the day. For instance, you could divide the first hour into 10 minute blocks for 'bits and pieces' such as opening and reading mail or addressing envelopes, and then move on to 30 minute blocks which give you time to work on bigger jobs such as writing an application, compiling a mailing list, or working on some aspect of your personal skills. Though such a timetable is worth setting up for all of your day, you can set one up only for the time you spend marketing yourself if you wish.

Now, look down your To Do list and work out how long it's going to take to finish each item on the list. If the job is going to take a number of hours, you might want to break it into smaller periods of time, rather than trying to do everything at once. After you have done this, start filling in the grid with the jobs that you have to do. Remember what you learned about being a lark or an owl and try and schedule your work load so you do the most difficult or complicated jobs when you are at your best. You can do the more boring and routine self-marketing jobs when you are winding down for the day, or have not yet got going.

If you are working on your self-marketing for a few hours at a time, then remember to fit some five or ten minute breaks into your timetable every 40 to 45 minutes or so. You will feel fresher and more mentally alert for it. During these periods you can either take a complete break or just do something different. The saying that a change is as good as a rest is absolutely right. However, don't go and do something that is going to take 20 minutes to finish during your five minute break, otherwise you'll be frustrated at having to leave it to go back to what you were doing, or worse still you'll finish the small job before getting back to what you really had to do.

MOTIVATING YOURSELF

Besides using lists and creating a timetable another good way of ensuring that you crank your self-marketing into top gear is to set **deadlines** for yourself. These are times by which you must have finished a job or a section of it. For example, you might tell yourself that you have to finish an application letter by 3 pm, or that you will have done research in the library on local companies by Thursday. When you set these deadlines, try to be realistic. If you aren't, you will miss them and become disillusioned and frustrated. When you make a deadline, write it down on a sheet of paper and pin this up in front of you to act as a reminder. Some people might like to go a step further by buying a clockwork timer and working against this to finish a job before it goes off.

Though deadlines are very useful tools for making you get on with your self-marketing you should use them carefully when you are doing anything that needs to be checked for spelling, grammer or factual detail. It is best not to work to a deadline for this type of work as more errors will creep in the faster you work.

Saving time on the phone
The telephone is a fantastic tool for self-marketing, if you know how to use it properly. If you don't then you will be less effective and waste valuable time.

- Make a list of all the calls that you are going to make in the day. Write down the person you want to speak to, the name of their company, their number and a few rough notes on what you are going to say. This will save you time by not having to hunt for numbers and names.

- Do your daily phone calls in a batch as much as possible. Once the phone is in your hand, don't put it down until you've finished making all the calls that you are going to do in that batch. This saves you quite a lot of time and stops you being distracted by something else between calls.

- During the telephone conversation jot down the main points that you want to remember. You can even use a tape recorder with a microphone that sticks to the receiver to do this. (You don't need to tell the other person you are recording the call unless you want to.)

- If people are busy when you call, don't hold on for them as this wastes time, but tell the receptionist that you will call them back. Don't be tempted to leave your name and number because this passes the initiative to the other person to call you back and you will just wait in disappointed expectation if they don't.

- If the call is one in which you need to be assertive or confident then make the call standing up. Also smile as you speak as this makes you sound more friendly.

- The phone deadens your voice, so try and animate it by making sure that you speak with highs and lows in your tone and not just in a flat voice.

Setting goals for yourself

You will make your self-marketing much easier if you set goals and targets for yourself. These can be a mixture of short and long term targets that you might achieve in a day, week, month or year.

Goals mean that at the end of every day you should be able to ask yourself 'What did I want to achieve today/this week/month/year?—Did I do it?'

Goals are good but you need to choose them with care if you are to get the most out of them, so your goals should be:

Specific

If they aren't you won't know what you're aiming for, or when you've reached it. So place actual numbers against them, for instance, your short term goals might be to make 15 self-marketing sales calls in the day, or write ten letters of application during the week. Your longer term goals might include achieving promotion to personal assistant in the next six months, or increasing your earnings by ten per cent in the next year.

Achievable

It's no good having unrealistic goals which you cannot possibly reach. Saying that you want to be so good at self-marketing that you will be chairman of a multi-national company within three months is not achievable.

Time limited

Whatever self-marketing goals you set for yourself each should have a time limit as this gives them a much needed urgency. Saying that you are going to send off 20 applications in the next week is very different from saying that you are going to mail the same number over the next two months.

When you have decided your goals you should write them down as this makes them more concrete and acts as a prompt to you. As you get better at goal setting you should set yourself increasingly difficult targets that force you to push yourself to achieve them.

DOING WHAT YOU WOULD LIKE TO PUT OFF

A Spanish proverb states that 'Tomorrow is the busiest day of the week'; well, it certainly can be if you continually put off doing the things that you have to do. Putting off doing things is called **procrastination** and it can be a real problem as situations only tend to get worse by not doing them. Some of the things that you might procrastinate over in your self-marketing programme could include updating your CV, revamping your wardrobe, or booking yourself onto a public speaking course.

These are some ideas to help you do the things that you have to do.

- Write down a time for starting or doing a certain job and be determined that you will do it at that time.

- If what you have to do will take a long time or is complicated, then break it down into smaller jobs which are more manageable and are easier to complete. These take less time to complete and will seem less daunting to you.

- Develop a rhythm by moving immediately from one self-marketing job to the next without giving yourself any time to think about stopping or putting off what you are about to do. If you programme yourself like a robot to do this you will achieve far more.

- After you have completed a job that you were putting off give yourself a small reward. This might be something as simple as making yourself a cup of coffee, taking a walk, or eating a slice of cake.

SELF-MARKETING FROM HOME

Many people have to do their self-marketing from home because they have nowhere else to do it from or for reasons of privacy or confidentiality. Looking for another job from work can be difficult. Now your home is obviously convenient, but there can be problems caused particularly by others and by the relaxed environment and nature of the home. These tips should help you overcome some of the difficulties that you might face.

- Create a place from which you will do all your self-marketing. This could be a study if there is one in the house, the dining room, or the spare bedroom. But wherever it is, you should try and make sure that you won't be disturbed.

- Impress upon your family how important it is to you and them that you are allowed to get on with the job of self-marketing without distraction or interruption. If you are unemployed then they should treat this as your job for now and let you get on with it. This means that when you are 'at work' like this they shouldn't take advantage of you by asking you to do little jobs for them, 'because it will only take a minute or so'.

● Get friends and neighbours out of the habit of just popping around for a chat or for a cup of coffee. You must learn to say 'no' to them. So, when they do come by, explain why you can't be disturbed right now and persuade them to phone you in future to find out when you'll be free, then they'll be saved the inconvenience of coming round and finding that you're unavailable.

Action plan

Start acquiring the habit of planning your day, whether it is a work day or a leisure day. The more you do this the easier it will become.

Identify ways in which you waste time regularly. Don't assume that the ways you waste time now will be the same ways that you waste time in a month or six months, so keep a check. Write down 20 ways in which you waste time:

1	11 . . . .
2	12 . . . .
3	13 . . . .
4	14 . . . .
5	15 . . . .
6	16 . . . .
7	17 . . . .
8	18 . . . .
9	19 . . . .
10	20 . . . .

Constantly look for new ways to motivate yourself:

Think of ten things that could motivate you. These could be little treats such as a piece of cake or trip to the cinema, or large rewards such as holidays or a new car:

1	6 . . . .
2	7 . . . .
3	8 . . . .
4	9 . . . .
5	10 . . . .

Develop the habit of making sure your desk is clear at the end of every day, not by sweeping everything into the drawers, but by making sure that all the work you intended to do has been done.

CASE HISTORY

Jan's timetable

This is the timetable that Jan has created for herself. She is unemployed and has a child who has just started school, giving Jan the chance to 'self-market' herself from 9.30 in the morning to 3.00, when she has to go and fetch her daughter. Notice how she still makes room for lunch when she takes a complete break and picks up her energy by having a wholesome lunch.

Daily timetable	**Date** _____	
Start	*To do*	*Duration*
		(minutes)
9.30	Open mail	10
9.40	Begin making notes for speculative job letter	30
10.10	Break	5
10.15	Begin writing letter	40
11.00	Phone companies to find name of personnel manager	10
11.10	Finish letter	40
11.40	Break	10
11.50	Start making notes for application received	30
12.20	Address envelopes for applications	20
12.40	Lunch	60

Fig. 10. Part of a daily timetable.

10
Marketing Yourself at Work

When you have got yourself a job, marketing yourself shouldn't stop there if you are going to make a success of your career. So in this chapter you will learn how effective self-marketing can push you further and faster up your career ladder.

LEARNING ABOUT A COMPANY

Information is power. And the more that you know about a prospective or existing employer the better, because this tells you whether they deserve your efforts or whether it is time to move on. So:

- Read as much as you can about the company including annual reports, brochures, newsletters past and present and newspaper cuttings. This information could be held at the library or made generally available from business agencies, such as the local Training and Enterprise Council (TEC). If the firm has a public relations department or press office, you could call them and ask for background information about the company. You can either be straightforward with them when you do this, or suggest that you are a freelance journalist if you want to be more devious. Alternatively the personnel department may be able to give you some information.

- If you are after a specific job, then you can phone the personnel department and ask them specifically about it while getting more information about the company at the same time. This hopefully should give you a better indication of how you might angle your CV or application in a way that is particularly relevant. Don't be afraid of doing this because there are a number of distinct advantages for you. First, you may well get through to the person who will be interviewing you. If so, then your call should give you a head start as they are likely to remember you and your initiative when they read your application or CV. And second, you may find out that you don't want to apply after all.

- Talk to people outside the company about what they know of it. Do the same with people inside the company.

- If the company is a local one, ask the local library if they have any cuttings about it. Many hold newspaper stories of what local companies are doing, especially if they are quite large.

- Ask other employees what they know about the company and its reputation. If you haven't yet joined the company, is there anyone you know, or that you can be introduced to, who actually works for the company?

When not to work for a company

Sometimes it can pay you not to work for a company, even if they offer you a job. After all, you don't want to be only a few weeks into a new job when the company suddenly goes bust. This could deal a severe blow to your self-marketing, especially if you have been unemployed for some time and were just beginning to regain your self confidence. These are some of the danger signs to look for:

Premises

What do the premises look like? Are they clean and tidy or in a state of disarray? A company that is cutting back on the maintenance and appearance of its premises may be having to concentrate all its finances on just keeping going. Remember, appearances can be important. Do you want to work for a company that has no pride in itself?

Vehicles

Do the company vehicles look good or are they untidy and dirty? Again finances may be being squeezed.

Environment

Does the company appear miserly or are the surroundings and its premises luxurious? It is always more pleasurable to work for a company that provides a nice environment rather than having to be huddled in a heatless hut in the middle of ploughed fields. But be warned—appearances can be deceptive. The company that seems to be spending a great deal of money on opulent furnishings and the trappings of success may be being mismanaged. After all, is that the best way for the company to be spending its money?

People

Are the people who work there cheerful, friendly and happy? If not, why not? Are the working conditions not what they seem? Is the management causing problems? Do the staff know something you don't?

Image

Do people speak well of the company? If they do then it has a good image. However, if people criticise the company and blame it for things then there may be fundamental problems. And it is worth remembering that the organisation's problems immediately become yours the moment you join it. Think of the reaction when people hear that someone works for the Inland Revenue, or for British Rail after a train strike.

Share options

A lot of larger companies issue share options which employees can buy into. Have they done so? If they have then it may show a long term commitment to the company because they think it is going places.

If you do join a company then periodically ask yourself these questions as circumstances change and formerly profitable companies slide towards the floor. If it reaches a point where you don't like the company any more then stop working for it. If you have to keep working there, then promise yourself that this is only a temporary measure and start looking for new opportunities. Don't listen to the moaning minnies who tell you that you're lucky to have a job and that you should stick with it even if you don't like it.

STARTING WITH A NEW COMPANY

You have already seen how first impressions count and this is no more true than when starting work for a new company. Indeed, this can be a situation where marketing yourself can be particularly crucial. Think of the times you may have got off on the wrong foot with someone. After that, isn't it incredibly difficult to make them change their minds about you, or for you to alter your impressions of them?

Planning your route to work
Before your first day, work out the best route for getting to and from work, including costings and any problems that you might have. Work out alternative routes. This will hopefully go a long way to ensuring that you don't turn up late on your first day and certainly not in the first few weeks.

Finding out who's who
Read the company newsletter if there is one, past and present issues. Put names and job titles to faces, then you will know who someone is without having to ask. If you can, contribute to the company newsletter by writing an article or sending in a letter; when this is published you start being a name in the company yourself.

Talking to colleagues
If the company doesn't have such a formal information sheet then ask work colleagues for pen portraits of people in the organisation, particularly those who are immediately above you or with whom you will have dealings on a regular basis. Cross reference and match what each one of them says about people so that you get a more balanced picture. The last thing you want is a distorted picture because of someone else's personal prejudice.

Building up a picture
At first get on as many distribution lists as you can. Read everything quickly for general interest and background and then read material that is of particular benefit more carefully. You will soon be able to take yourself off some of the lists when you find the ones that are still valuable but at this stage you are really just trying to soak up the atmosphere and background of the company.

Networking

Join groups within the company. Get to know people. Listen to the gossip, but never gossip yourself. Network with people and learn to get on with superiors, but don't go sucking up to them.

Finding yourself a niche

Learn everything you can about one or two particular aspects of the company you have joined. This doesn't have to be one of the glamorous elements of the company, but it should be one of the most valuable areas of the business. If you become an expert on this area then very soon people will come to you for advice. This will make you noticeable and different from others in the company.

Looking for opportunities to shine

Do more than you are asked to do, though beware of overload. Take on little pet projects that will help the department or your boss. But be modest about your efforts. Don't flaunt them in front of others or your boss, but show them what you have done in parts (if appropriate) and at a suitable time when they will make more impact.

Taking training seriously

Start looking for training opportunities in the company and take them when offered.

Standing out from the crowd

Make yourself different by becoming famous within your company, so look for some relatively minor rule that you can break without penalty, perhaps an unwritten rule about the way that everyone should dress. Or you could generate a personal conflict with one of the company 'bad guys'. Such things soon get round the office grapevine and very soon you are a name within the organisation rather than just a number. Organising a charity event is a surefire way to raise your profile. First, the event is seen as being a good thing in its own right and something that all of the corporate bigwigs will want to be seen to be involved in; they will make sure that the person organising the event knows it. You can cut your way through layers of bureaucracy in double quick time.

Adapting to change

Be flexible and realistic in your approach to your work and your work colleagues. Be prepared to change tack if necessary to accommodate changes that are happening in the company.

Your attempts at self-marketing may seem painfully slow to yield results at first, and don't expect your career path to be always the direct one, or to go exactly along the lines that you have planned. Be patient. You must give your company the chance to deliver the goods. Though at some point you must ask yourself honestly whether those goods are ever going to arrive.

Keeping an office book

Nobody likes feeling foolish and yet when you start a new job or move into a different part of a large company it is all too easy to forget new procedures especially when **everything is new**. Just as you used a notebook to recall information on other people, making it look as though you have a superb memory, you can do the same around the office. So, in another notebook write down all the different office procedures, such as when mail has to be posted by, how the photocopier works, who holds the stationery key and anything else that you think might be useful. This is your book so don't be worried about writing down trivial items.

You can also use another office book to make basic notes about people, such as whether they are married, their wife or husband's name, how many children they have and their names, the sports and leisure activities they pursue. Look through these notes regularly so that the information stays fresh in your mind. Do this particularly before you have meetings with people. Any new information that comes to light during those meetings you should jot down immediately afterwards and add it to your notes. Be discreet about these notes and don't leave them lying about where colleagues may find them. If you are keeping innocuous notes about them then this may only give the game away about your 'superb memory', but if you keep more detailed and personal notes about them (such as their attitudes towards others, their general personality and the like) then it is very important that you keep these notes out of the way. If you don't and they are discovered, you will not be the most popular person around!

SELF-MARKETING WITH COLLEAGUES

Your work colleagues can make or break you, especially if you are expected to work as part of a team. Therefore it pays dividends to work as effectively and as productively with them as you can. A good rapport with and backing from colleagues can be very important in marketing yourself to bosses.

- Don't go out of your way to create enemies or rub colleagues up the wrong way. Try to get on well with everybody, but do your best not to take sides in a dispute unless you have to, or unless you are pretty confident about being on the winning side.

- Get your work done on time so that others aren't left with a work overload. They will blame you.

- Likewise make sure that you do the work properly. If you don't then others will have to pick up the pieces and again you won't be winning any popularity contests.

- Be a comfortable and approachable person whom others like to have around. If you always seem aloof then people won't tell you things that it might be in your interest to know, they won't help you out if you need it and they won't give you the support you deserve and require.

- If you are asked for help give it whenever possible. Look upon this as a savings account of goodwill on which you can draw at a later date by asking others for help. However, beware of overload.

Preventing overload

When trying to impress others with your enthusiasm and desire to succeed, don't overload yourself by taking on more than you can cope with. If you end up saying 'yes' to everything, then there is a very real chance that you will become less effective. Everything you do, including the more important work, will end up being rushed. And a job done badly will reflect on you—a black mark against your name. It is nearly always a mistake to equate long hours with success, though there is an element of truth in that. If you are continually working ten or 12 hours to impress the boss the chances are that you aren't working intelligently, probably you don't have very good time management techniques (see chapter 9). Working long hours does tend to be a mistake because the longer you work the less effective and efficient you become and the more mistakes you make. This does no one any good, least of all you. You should also be wary about giving help to others if they are going to claim the reward for it, or if you might be a fall guy if things go wrong, or when the time taken to help doesn't offer sufficient rewards for your efforts.

Dealing with a bad situation

No matter how good you are at a job, from time to time something will go wrong. An order will go astray, a report won't be completed on time or a client will feel they have been mistreated. Bad situations you just have to accept but the good self-marketer will still try and use them to the fullest advantage.

- If things go wrong and you are to blame, then take responsibility for what you have done. Don't try and blame others or make excuses, though you should try to explain your reasons for doing or not doing something.

- If you have made a mistake then try and put right the damage as soon as you can.

- If the problem lies with someone else then do your best not to drop them in it. This will mark you out as someone who can't be trusted by colleagues. It is better to say that you don't know the details of a situation.

ARE YOU IN THE RIGHT JOB?

One of the occasions when you will be particularly interested in marketing yourself is when you are on the look out for a new job. Most of us find that after we have been in a job for a while we find that we may have outgrown it or changed so much that it no longer gives us any pleasure. Is your job still right for you?

- Are you increasingly thinking that the customers are idiots?

- Are you increasingly thinking that your boss is an idiot?

- Are you having to work longer and longer hours?

- Are you being asked to do things that you don't like doing and which you never expected to do when you took the job on?

- Are you becoming bored with the work that you have to do?

- Is the strain of travelling becoming too much?

- Do you have that Monday morning feeling every day of the week?

- Is working becoming increasingly pressurised?

- Are you finding it more and more difficult to work with your colleagues?

- Are you having too much responsibility for too little reward?

- Are you being paid too little for what you do?

- Has the work become unsuitable for your changing personality?

If you had the choice who would you like to work for?

. . . .
. . . .

Why would you like to work for them? Give six reasons.

1   . . . .
2   . . . .
3   . . . .
4   . . . .
5   . . . .
6   . . . .

If you are employed, does your current company provide these reasons? If not why not?

. . . .
. . . .
. . . .
. . . .

CASE HISTORIES

Anna stops being a doormat

Anna works for a firm of publishers. She is a creative person, but a little naive and modest about her abilities. Perhaps under normal circumstances this wouldn't have mattered, but unfortunately for Anna, she has a colleague, Michael, a rather opinionated and arrogant young man who, though not as talented as Anna, knows how to work the system. For example, several times Anna talked over ideas with Michael, who managed to dissuade her from submitting them, only to find those same ideas presented to her boss by Michael as though they were his own. Anna knew she couldn't say anything without appearing to suffer from a case of sour grapes, and anyway she had no proof that the idea was hers. To spike Michael's guns she decided that she would start playing rougher with him. So, just as she had done before, Anna discussed a couple of ideas with Michael. Again he was very negative towards them. But unknown to Michael, Anna had thoroughly researched and written up her ideas, and had already presented them to the department head. At the meeting Michael presented the ideas only to find himself having a private meeting with his boss, and a stern warning never to steal ideas again.

Sally makes the best of a bad job

Sally is dissatisfied with her job. Some redundancies have recently been made and the atmosphere in the company isn't good even though the business is now on a more secure financial footing. What is more, Sally has a new boss with whom she is not getting on well. She is of course looking for a new job, but knows that it may be some months before she lands a new one, so she decides that she is going to make the best of the situation by looking for new ways to make her present job more satisfying. So rather than just doing what she has to do, she does a little more: taking on some extra work from the marketing department, getting involved with the group that is looking to change the existing word-processing software. After a couple of months of doing this Sally has learned quite a lot that she didn't know before. Her boss is impressed and mellows in his attitude towards her. Sally is even offered a new position within the marketing department because of her recent efforts. But though she has made the last couple of months enjoyable for herself, Sally decides that enough is enough and moves elsewhere when a suitable job comes up.

Glossary

Active listening Not just hearing but really listening to what another person is saying so that you obtain a better understanding of the speaker's feelings, emotions and the messages behind their words.

Assertiveness Essentially standing up for your rights in a firm but non-aggressive manner.

Body language The messages that our bodies give off and which are picked up consciously and subconsciously by others. Body language is communicated through the way we stand, gesture, move and through facial expression.

Closed questions Questions that tend to require a yes or no response. For example, 'Can you type?'

Effectiveness Doing the right thing at the right time.

Efficiency Doing something without waste or effort. You can do the wrong thing efficiently, therefore it is better to be effective rather than efficient.

Effort The amount of energy and commitment you put into any task or job.

Eye contact Keeping your eyes fixed on the other person, but not staring at them. Maintaining eye contact is a good way of showing someone that you are interested in what they are saying.

Goals Targets you set yourself and attempt to reach. Goals are important in giving your life and work a purpose. They also show you how successful you are in marketing yourself.

Hidden agenda The motives and reasons for people doing things, but which you do not know about. You will not fully understand why someone is behaving in the way they do if you do not know their hidden motives.

High flyer Someone who is heading for the top of their profession.

Image The particular picture you show the world. Your image depends upon the way you speak, behave and dress. You can have a number of different images.

Interview A formal meeting and conversation between at least two people, very often to assess an applicant's suitability for a job.

Jargon Specialised language that many people use when talking or writing about their own subject. Though jargon provides a short cut when communicating with people in your own field, it is more difficult for the 'outsider' to understand what you are talking about.

Lateral thinking A way of thinking which means that you look at a problem not from straight ahead, but from other angles and directions.

Maverick Someone who is not one of the crowd, but tends to kick against the system and cause a stir.

Media The press, television and radio.

Mentor An experienced and trusted person who can help someone who is less experienced and knowledgeable.

Motivation The reason(s) why people do things.

Networking Making a conscious effort to meet people who will be able to provide you with information, advice and further contacts which will help you move forward in your career.

Non-verbal communication The same as body language.

Office book A notebook in which you keep information relating to office procedures and data. This serves as a central reference source and is very useful when you start a new job.

Open questions Questions which require more than a basic yes or no answer. For example, 'How would you deal with an awkward customer?'

Passive listening Physically hearing what others are saying, but not really listening so that you don't fully understand what they are talking about or interpret their emotions. In effect, 'listening with half an ear'.

Procrastination Putting off doing what you have to do.

Public relations Doing the things that make you appear in the best possible way to those around you and to the press.

'Salami' technique Chopping up a problem or task into slices so that it becomes more manageable to cope with.

Self-management Techniques and attitudes that help you take control of your life.

Self-marketing Techniques and attitudes that help you promote yourself in the best and most effective way possible.

Specific skills Skills that are closely linked with an industry or type of job. For example, knowing how to operate a particular type of machine in the plastics industry would be a specific skill.

Stress Excessive tension that can lead to health problems.

Time management Organising the time available to you so that you achieve the most within that time.

Transportable skills Skills that are of use in a number of careers and jobs: for example, selling and keyboard skills.

Underselling Not emphasising your skills, experience or background sufficiently to others, through modesty or inadequate self-marketing.

Further Reading

IMAGE MAKING

A gentleman's wardrobe, Paul Keers (Weidenfeld).
The complete style guide (for women), Mary Spillane (Piatkus).
The professional image (for women), Susan Bixler (Putnam).
Presenting yourself for men, Mary Spillane (Piatkus).
Presenting yourself for women, Mary Spillane (Piatkus).

VOICE IMPROVEMENT AND PUBLIC SPEAKING

How to talk so people listen, Sonya Hamlin (Thorsons).
Powerspeak, Dorothy Leeds (Piatkus).
How to master public speaking, Anne Nichols (How To Books).
Present yourself, Michael Gelb (Aurium).

WRITING SKILLS

How to write business letters, Ann Dobson (How To Books).
How to master business English, Michael Bennie (How To Books).
Write right, Jan Venolia (David & Charles).
Writing to win, Mel Lewis (McGraw Hill).
How to write a CV that works, Paul McGee (How To Books).
How to write a report, John Bowden (How To Books).
How to write articles for profit and PR, Mel Lewis (Kogan Page).
Put it in writing, John Whale (Dent).

SELF MANAGEMENT

Personal power, Phillipa Davies (Piatkus).
A manager's guide to self development, Pedler, Burgoyne & Boydell (McGraw Hill).
How to manage your career, Roger Jones (How To Books).
Body language, Jane Lyle (Hamlyn).
Awaken the giant within, Anthony Robbins (Simon and Schuster).
Unlimited power, Anthony Robbins (Simon and Schuster).

TIME MANAGEMENT

Manage your time, Sally Garret (Fontana).
Getting things done, Roger Black (Michael Joseph).

INTERVIEWS AND APPLICATIONS

The interview game—and how it's played, Celia Roberts (BBC Publications).
CVs and written applications, Judy Skeats (Ward Lock).
Mid-career action guide, Derek and Fred Kemp (Kogan Page).
How to pass that interview, Judith Johnstone (How To Books).

EDUCATION

How to study and learn, Peter Marshall (How To Books).
Never too late to learn, Bell & Roderick (Longman).
Open learning directory, (The Training Agency).
Occupations 95, (Careers & Occupations Information).

Useful Addresses

The Federation of Image Consultants, 78 Blois Lane, Chesham, Buckinghamshire HP 6 6BZ. Tel: (01494) 4320138.

University of the Third Age, 1 Stockwell Green, London SW9 9JF.

The Open University, Walton Hall, Milton Keynes MK7 6AA. Tel: (01908) 274066.

Society of Teachers of Speech and Drama, 73 Berry Hill Road, Mansfield, Nottinghamshire NG18 4RU.

Society of Teachers of the Alexander Technique, 20 London House, 266 Fulham Road, London SW10 9EL. Tel: (0171) 351 0828. (The Alexander Technique is concerned with improving the general posture of the body in a way which will give you more energy, confidence and relaxation.)

The Association for Stammerers, St Margaret's House, 21 Old Ford Street, Bethnal Green, London E2 9PL. Tel: (0181) 983 1003.

Index

How to Write Business Letters
Ann Dobson

Without proper help, lots of people find it quite hard to cope with even basic business correspondence. Intended for absolute beginners, this book uses fictional characters in a typical business setting to contrast the right and wrong ways to go about things. Taking nothing for granted, the book shows how to plan a letter, how to write and present it, how to deal with requests, how to write and answer complaints, standard letters, personal letters, job applications, letters overseas, and a variety of routine and tricky letters. Good, bad and middling examples are used, to help beginners see for themselves the right and wrong ways of doing things. Ann Dobson is principal of a secretarial training school with long experience of helping people improve their business skills.

160pp illus. 1 85703 104 0.

How to Write a Report
John Bowden

Communicating effectively on paper is an essential skill for today's business or professional person. Written by an experienced manager and staff trainer, this well-presented handbook provides a very clear step-by-step framework for every individual, whether dealing with professional colleagues, customers, clients, suppliers or junior or senior staff. Contents: Preparation and planning. Collecting and handling information. Writing the report: principles and techniques. Improving your thinking. Improving presentation. Achieving a good writing style. Making effective use of English. How to choose and use illustrations. Choosing paper, covers and binding. Appendices (examples, techniques, checklists), glossary, index. 'Most of us have a need to write report of some kind at various times, and this book has real value . . . Thoroughly commendable.' *IPS Journal*. John Bowden BSc(Econ) MSc has long experience both as a professional manger in industry, and as a Senior Lecturer running courses in accountancy, auditing and effective communication.

160pp illus. 1 85703 124 5. Second edition

How to Master Public Speaking
Anne Nicholls

Speaking well in public is one of the most useful skills any of us can acquire. Whether you are a nervous novice or a practised pro, this step-by-step handbook tells you everything you need to know to master this highly prized communication skill. 'In addition to usefulness of content, the book has attractiveness of print, paper and binding to recommend it.' *Spoken English*. 'I found this book an excellent read and recommend it wholeheartedly. It is full of helpful practical information.' *Phoenix/Association of Graduate Careers Advisory Services*. 'Especially welcome is the constant stress on the needs of the audience being of paramount importance . . . A good deal to recommend it.' *Speech & Drama*.

160pp illus. 1 85703 149 0. Third edition.

How to Master Business English
Michael Bennie

Are you communicating effectively? Do your business documents achieve the results you want? Or are they too often ignored or misunderstood? Good communication is the key to success in any business. Whether you are trying to sell a product, answer a query or complaint, or persuade colleagues, the way you express yourself is often as important as what you say. With lost of examples, checklists and questionnaires to help you, the new edition of this book will speed you on your way. 'An excellent book—not in the least dull . . . Altogether most useful for anyone seeking to improve their communication skills.' *IPS Journal*. 'Gives guidance on writing styles for every situation . . . steers the reader through the principles and techniques of effective letter-writing and document-planning.' *First Voice*. 'Useful chapters on grammar, punctuation and spelling. Frequent questionnaires and checklists enable the reader to check progress.' *Focus (Society of Business Teachers)*. 'The language and style is easy to follow . . . Excellent value for money.' *Spoken English*.

208pp illus. 1 85703 129 6. Second edition.

How to Pass that Interview
Judith Johnstone

Everyone knows how to shine at interviews—or do they? When every candidate becomes the perfect clone of the one before, you have to have that extra 'something' to raise your chances above the rest. Using a systematic and practical approach, this **How To** book takes you step-by-step through the essential pre-interview ground-work, the interview encounter itself, and what you can learn from the experience afterwards. The book contains sample pre- and post-interview correspondence, and is complete with a guide to further reading, glossary of terms, and index. 'This is from the first class How To Books stable.' *Escape Committee Newsletter.* 'Offers a fresh approach to a well documented subject.' *Newscheck/ Careers Service Bulletin.* 'A complete step-by-step guide.' *The Association of Business Executives.* Judith Johnstone is a Graduate of the Institute of Personnel & Development; she has been an instructor in Business Studies and adult literacy tutor, and has long experience of helping people at work.

128pp illus. 1 85703 118 0. Second edition.

How to Manage Your Career
Roger Jones

Would you like a great career, with real job satisfaction, generous pay and conditions? Lots of people already enjoy such careers—and so could you if you manage things in the right way. But how do you 'market' yourself? How do you handle job interviews? How do you negotiate and interact with colleagues? And how do you solve problems concerning personal relationships, harassment or discrimination? Should you work for yourself, or perhaps move overseas? In the fast-changing 1990s, developing a successful working life calls for constant attention, learning, and a willingness to adapt. Study the valuable advice in this positive and forward-looking book. Take change of yourself—and your future. Roger Jones BA MInstAM MIM is a leading author, writer and lecturer on careers topics. His other books include *How to Get a Job Abroad, How to Master Languages* and others in this Series.

160pp illus. 1 85703 107 5.

How to Study & Learn
Peter Marshall

Are you thinking of studying or training for an important qualification? Do you know the right techniques for studying and learning, to ensure you achieve the best results as quickly as possible? Whether you are at college or university, doing projects and assignments, writing essays, receiving continuous assessment or preparing for exams, this is the book for you. In practical steps it covers getting your thinking right, organising yourself properly, finding and processing the information you need, reading effectively, developing good writing skills, thinking creatively, motivating yourself, and more. Whatever your subject, age or background, start now—and turn yourself into a winning candidate. Peter Marshall BA BSc (Econ) has a wealth of experience as a university and college teacher, both in the UK and abroad.

160pp illus. 1 85703 062 1.

How to Apply for a Job
Judith Johnstone

Tough new realities are dominating the jobs market. It is no longer enough to send employers lists of worthy past achievements or vague details of hobbies and 'interests'. Employers want to know: 'What skills can you offer? What can you do for us, and how fast? What personal commitment will you put on the line? What value for money will you be?' Whether you are short term or long term unemployed, a school or college leaver, or mature returner to the workplace, this book shows you how to clarify what you can really offer, and how to market this effectively to meet an employment need. 'Very practical and informative.' *Phoenix/Association of Graduate Careers Advistory Services.*

160pp illus. 1 85703 138 5. Second edition.